CHELSEA IN 50 BUILDINGS

LUCY McMURDO

AMBERLEY

First published 2025

Amberley Publishing, The Hill, Stroud
Gloucestershire GL5 4EP

www.amberley-books.com

British Library Cataloguing in Publication Data.
A catalogue record for this book is available from the British Library.

ISBN 978 1 3981 2091 4 (print)
ISBN 978 1 3981 2092 1 (ebook)

Typesetting by SJmagic DESIGN SERVICES, India.
Printed in Great Britain.

Appointed GPSR EU Representative: Easy Access System Europe Oü, 16879218
Address: Mustamäe tee 50, 10621, Tallinn, Estonia
Contact Details: gpsr.requests@easproject.com, +358 40 500 3575

Contents

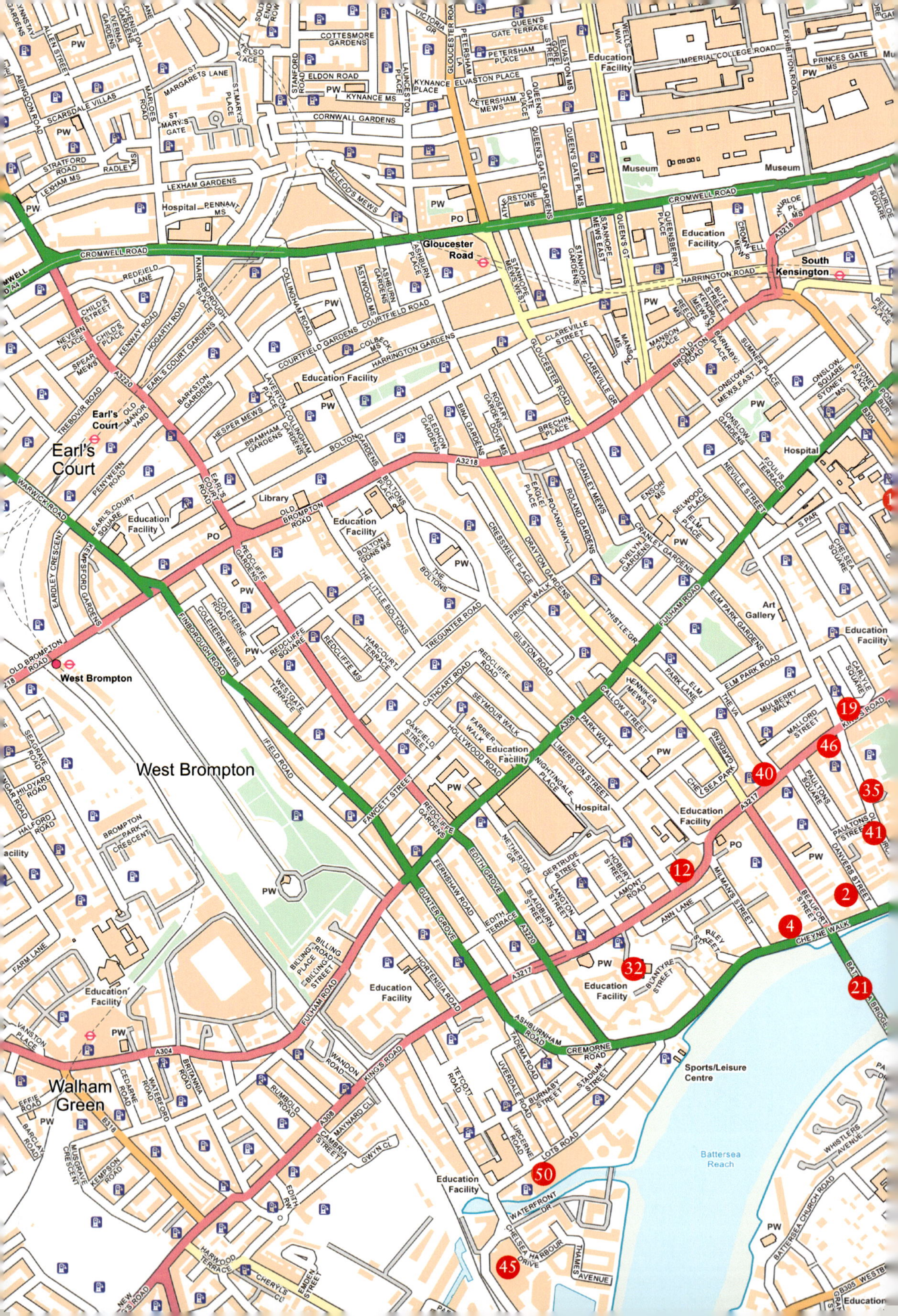

Cottesmore Gardens
Queen's Gate Terrace
Imperial College Road
Princes Gate
Exhibition Road
Education Facility
Petersham Place
Elvaston Place
Kynance Place
Kynance Ms
Eldon Road
Cornwall Gardens
Scarsdale Villas
St Mary's Gate
St Margarets Lane
Stratford Road
Radley Ms
Lexham Ms
Lexham Gardens
Hospital
Pennant Ms
McLeod's Mews
Museum
Cromwell Road
Gloucester Road
Harrington Road
South Kensington
Thurloe Pl Ms
Thurloe Square
Queensberry Place
Courtfield Gardens
Courtfield Road
Harrington Gardens
Colbeck Ms
Knaresborough Place
Collingham Road
Redfield Lane
Child's Street
Child's Place
Nevern Place
Kenway Road
Hogarth Road
Spear Mews
Earl's Court Gardens
Trebovir Road
Earl's Court
Old Manor Yard
Barkston Gardens
Hesper Mews
Bramham Gardens
Laverton Place
Collingham Gardens
Bolton Gardens
Penywern Road
Warwick Road
Earl's Court Square
Library
Old Brompton Road
Boltons Place
The Boltons
Bolton Gdns Ms
The Little Boltons
Gledhow Gardens
Bina Gardens
Rosary Gardens
Dove Ms
Brechin Place
Clareville Street
Clareville Gr
Old Brompton Road
Onslow Mews East
Onslow Gardens
Onslow Square
Sumner Place
Sydney Place
Sydney Ms
Foulis Terrace
Neville Street
Selwood Place
Elm Place
Cranley Gardens
Cranley Mews
Roland Gardens
Roland Way
Eagle Place
Evelyn Gardens
Ensor Ms
Cresswell Place
Drayton Gardens
Priory Walk
Thistle Gr
Fulham Road
Elm Park Gardens
Elm Park Road
Art Gallery
Chelsea Square
Carlyle Square
Mulberry Walk
Mallord Street
The Vale
Park Lane
Elm Park Lane
Eardley Crescent
Kempsford Gardens
Redcliffe Gardens
Coleherne Road
Coleherne Mews
Redcliffe Square
Redcliffe Ms
Harcourt Terrace
Tregunter Road
Gilston Road
Cathcart Road
Redcliffe Road
Seymour Walk
Oakfield Street
Farrier Walk
Hollywood Road
Limerston Street
Park Walk
Callow Street
Hennicker Mews
Chelsea Park Gardens
West Brompton
Westgate Terrace
Ifield Road
Finborough Road
Fawcett Street
Nightingale Place
Netherton Gr
Gertrude Street
Hobury Street
Lamont Road
Langton Street
Milman's Street
Riley Street
Ann Lane
Beaufort Street
Paultons Square
Paultons Street
Danvers Street
Cheyne Walk
Battersea Bridge
King's Road
Seagrave Road
Hildyard Road
Halford Road
Brompton Park Crescent
Farm Lane
Vanston Place
Edith Grove
Edith Terrace
Fernshaw Road
Gunter Grove
Hortensia Road
Billing Road
Billing Place
Billing Street
Fulham Road
Blaidburn Street
Blantyre Street
Ashburnham Road
Cremorne Road
Sports/Leisure Centre
Walham Green
Effie Road
Barclay Road
Cedarne Road
Waterford Road
Britannia Road
Rumbold Road
Wandon Road
Maynard Cl
Cambria Street
Gwyn Cl
Tetcott Road
Uverdale Road
Tadema Road
Burnaby Street
Stadium Street
Upcerne Road
Lots Road
Battersea Reach
Whistlers Avenue
Battersea Church Road
Musgrave Crescent
Kempson Road
Edith Rw
Waterfront Dr
Chelsea Harbour Drive
Thames Avenue
Harwood Terrace
Cherlys Cl
Emden Street
A3218
A3220
A3217
A308
A304
A4
B304
B305
B318
PW
PO
19
46
40
35
41
12
2
4
32
21
50
45

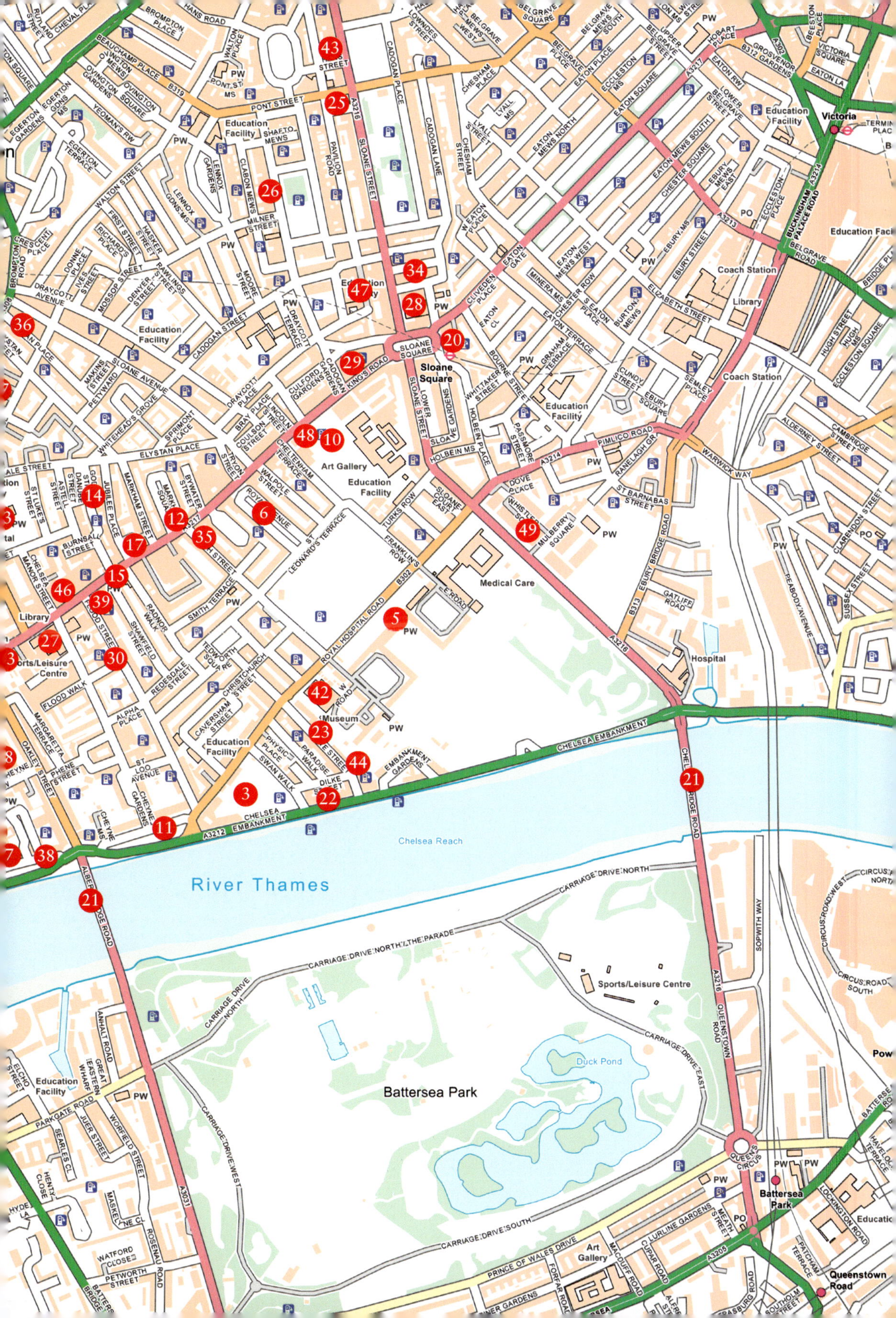

Victoria
Sloane Square
River Thames
Chelsea Reach
Battersea Park
Duck Pond
Sports/Leisure Centre
Battersea Park
Queenstown Road
Art Gallery
Education Facility
Medical Care
Hospital
Museum
Library
Coach Station
Chelsea Embankment
Carriage Drive North
Carriage Drive South
Carriage Drive East
Carriage Drive West
Queenstown Road
Chelsea Bridge Road
Albert Bridge Road
Royal Hospital Road
King's Road
Sloane Street
Pimlico Road
Ebury Bridge Road
Buckingham Palace Road
Belgrave Road
Warwick Way
Eaton Square
Chester Square
Cadogan Place
Cadogan Square
Pont Street
Sloane Avenue
Draycott Avenue
Cheyne Walk
Flood Street
Oakley Street
Tite Street
Swan Walk
Prince of Wales Drive
Parkgate Road
Queens Circus
Sopwith Way
Circus Road West
Circus Road South

Key

1. Chelsea Old Church, No. 64 Cheyne Walk, SW3
2. Crosby Moran Hall, Cheyne Walk, SW3
3. Chelsea Physic Garden, No. 66 Royal Hospital Road, SW3
4. Lindsey House, Nos 95–101 Cheyne Walk, SW3
5. The Royal Hospital Chelsea, Royal Hospital Road, SW3
6. Royal Avenue, Chelsea, SW3
7. Riverside Pubs: The Cross Keys and No. Fifty Cheyne, SW3
8. Carlyle's House, No. 24 Cheyne Row, SW3
9. Argyll House, Nos 211–17 King's Road, SW3
10. Duke of York Square, Royal Military Asylum and the Saatchi Gallery, SW3
11. Cheyne Walk, SW3
12. King's Road Boutiques: Mary Quant and Vivienne Westwood
13. St Luke's and Christchurch, Sydney Street, SW3
14. Godfrey Street and Chelsea Green, SW3
15. Chelsea Potter Pub, No. 119 King's Road, SW3
16. Chelsea Hospitals, Sydney Street and the Fulham Road, SW3
17. The Pheasantry, No. 152 King's Road, SW3
18. Glebe Place, SW3
19. The Cadogan Arms, No. 298 King's Road, SW3
20. The Royal Court Theatre, Sloane Square, SW3
21. River Crossings: Battersea, Chelsea and Albert Bridges, SW3
22. Norman Shaw Buildings, Nos 9–17 Chelsea Embankment, SW3
23. Tite Street Houses: Artistic and Literary Hub, SW3
24. Carlyle Mansions, Cheyne Walk, SW3
25. Cadogan Hotel, No. 75 Sloane Street, SW3
26. Hans Town and Cadogan Square, SW1
27. Chelsea Old Town Hall, Nos 165–179 King's Road, SW3
28. Holy Trinity Church, Sloane Street, SW3
29. Peter Jones Department Store, Sloane Square, SW3
30. Flood Street Studios: Nos 1–11 and No. 72 Flood Street, SW3
31. Church of Our Most Holy Redeemer and St Thomas More, Upper Cheyne Row, SW3
32. World's End and the World's End Estate, King's Road, SW3
33. The Ivy Chelsea Garden, No. 197 King's Road, SW3
34. Cadogan Hall, No. 5 Sloane Terrace, SW1
35. Nos 46 and 46c Old Church Street and No. 69 King's Road
36. Michelin House, No. 81 Fulham Road, SW3
37. Samuel Lewis and Sutton Trust Estates, Ixworth Place, SW3
38. Cabmen's Shelter, Chelsea Embankment, SW3
39. Former Temperance Billiard Hall, Nos 131–141 King's Road, and Motorcar Garage, No. 15 Flood Street, SW3
40. The Bluebird Restaurant, No. 350, King's Road, SW3
41. Old Church Street, SW3
42. National Army Museum, Royal Hospital Road, SW3
43. Royal Danish Embassy, Sloane Street, SW1
44. The Red House, No. 37 Tite Street, SW3
45. Chelsea Harbour and Imperial Wharf, SW10
46. King's Road Cinemas, SW3
47. Pavilion Road, SW1
48. Vardo, Duke of York Square, SW3
49. Chelsea Barracks, Chelsea Bridge Road, SW1
50. Powerhouse at Chelsea Waterfront (former Lots Road Power Station), SW10

Introduction

The King's Road is the very heart of Chelsea today, yet it was once King Charles II's private road which allowed him safe passage from London to Hampton Court Palace. It is known worldwide for its fabulous designer and independent shops and is greatly associated with fashion, music, food, art, film, the motorcar and, of course, the 'swinging sixties'. In the mid-twentieth century it was a real mecca for young people, a place 'where anything goes', clothes were both revolutionary and outrageous, and designers like Mary Quant and Vivienne Westwood thrived. It was home to and frequented by artists, intellectuals, musicians, actors and every type of bohemian in London. At weekends King's Road was heaving with youngsters mincing up and down its pavements and visiting shops like the Chelsea Drugstore, I Was Lord Kitchener's Thing and John Michael. Having established a revolution in clothing – the miniskirt, high boots, latex outfits and all manner of punk paraphernalia – the King's Road in the twenty-first century seems much quieter and less frenetic, maybe even a little sedate in comparison. However, it is still very much the place to be seen and to enjoy the café culture, the splendid many and varied eateries and bars and the chic individual shops and boutiques. Much of Chelsea comes under the portfolio of the Cadogan Estate, the Cadogans having been landowners here since the eighteenth century. They have been great philanthropists in the area and are responsible for many of the changes that have occurred over the centuries. In recent years the estate has revitalised Cadogan Hall, transforming it into a concert hall and events venue; commissioned the building of the Duke of York Square; renovated and re-established Pavilion Road as an artisanal quarter; and brought about a new arts and cultural hub at the Gaumont building.

The building of Hans Town with its magnificent red-brick Continental canal-style architecture was largely due to the 5th Earl of Cadogan's support in the late 1800s, and its Queen Anne Revival design is now an established feature of Chelsea. All throughout the nineteenth century the fields and pastureland in and around the King's Road were replaced by streets and housing as Chelsea's population grew. Today, if you turn down any of its side streets you will find rows of delightful Georgian houses as well as handsome squares. Some of the smaller terraces, originally artisan homes, are now extremely expensive properties and are widely sought after. These have been made all the more popular since the reality TV programme *Made in Chelsea* was first broadcast in 2011. The series, following the everyday lives of affluent Chelsea youngsters, has promoted many of the neighbourhood's cafés, bars and restaurants.

Yet Chelsea has always attracted people for its entertainment and recreational activities. Crowds would flock to its pleasure gardens at Ranelagh and Cremorne in the eighteenth and nineteenth centuries, and to its inns and taverns, especially those beside the river. Nowadays, Chelsea draws in people to its restaurants and nightlife, but they also come to visit the Saatchi Gallery, National Army Museum, the Royal Hospital Chelsea and the Chelsea Physic Garden. The latter, bordering Chelsea Embankment, is more than 350 years old and contains many medicinal and exotic plants in a wonderful walled garden setting.

Nearby, the annual Chelsea Flower Show is held in the gardens of the Royal Hospital Chelsea, an institution set up by Charles II in the early 1680s as a home for wounded veterans (today known as the Chelsea Pensioners) of the regular army. During the show huge numbers of the shops and local businesses decorate their windows with floral displays, and floral tableaux are erected in Sloane Square and along the King's Road, enhancing the buildings and the district itself.

It is hard to imagine this wealthy London village as ever having been different, but it was a poor riverside community for many years and a cheap place to live. Many artists set up home here, benefiting from the area's inexpensive rents and from their proximity to the Thames, the beauty of which they were keen to capture in their paintings. Chelsea became established as London's artistic centre, with Whistler, Turner, Sargent, Rossetti and Greaves amongst others making it their

Royal Avenue during the Chelsea Flower Show.

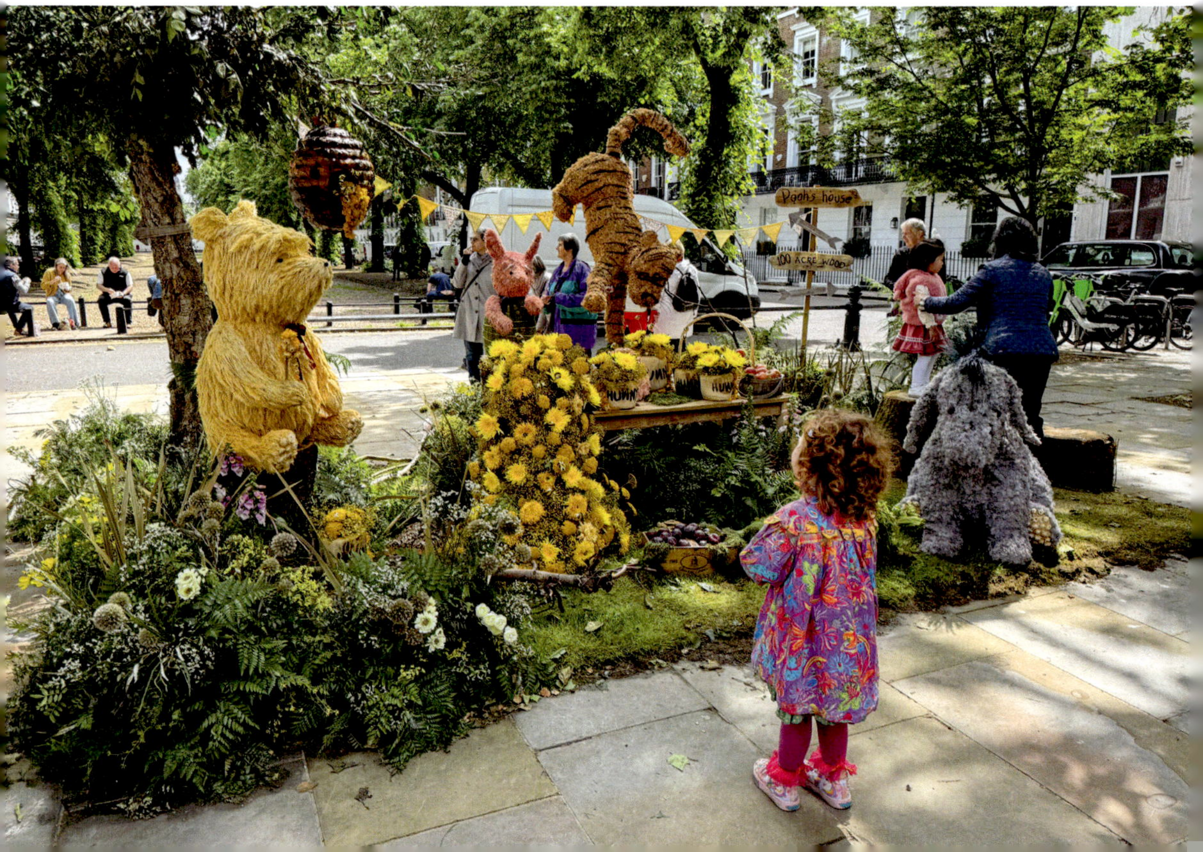

home. In the 1890s Chelsea Arts Club moved into Old Church Street while the artists themselves settled into houses and studios in nearby Cheyne Walk, Manresa Road, Flood Street and Glebe Place. Nowadays, Old Church Street contains one of Chelsea's most expensive properties, Sloane House, owned by Petra Ecclestone and her husband, Sam Palmer. The street also contains two modernist homes built in the 1930s which are a testament to the architectural period. Along the street at No. 127 is a blue plaque to William and Evelyn de Morgan. Although both were artists, William had previously run a pottery in Cheyne Walk and was a remarkable ceramicist. Interestingly, he was continuing Chelsea's link to pottery-making that had begun a century earlier with the Chelsea porcelain factory.

Throughout the nineteenth and twentieth centuries Chelsea was associated with some of the country's best-known writers, its aesthetes, architects and intellectuals. Oscar Wilde, T. S. Eliot, Somerset Maugham, Henry James and George Eliot were Chelsea residents and many celebrity footballers, rock stars, politicians, entrepreneurs and even the suffragette Sylvia Pankhurst have made the village their home too. The impact of architects such as R. Norman Shaw, Ernest George and G. A. Peto on Chelsea's architecture cannot be ignored either.

Unsurprisingly, Chelsea's reputation as an enclave of the affluent and influential is not new. It was here around 500 years ago that Sir Thomas More and then King Henry VIII built mansion houses overlooking the river. At that time Chelsea was rural, an area of fields, market gardens and orchards far away from the bustle, stench and pollution of the City of London. People mainly travelled here by boat along London's highway, the River Thames, and enjoyed Chelsea as a retreat, taking pleasure in its clean air and picturesque riverside. In the sixteenth century Chelsea was little more than a village and its residents lived and worked either close to the river or tended pasture and market gardens inland. St Luke's Church was the parish church for the small community and included amongst its congregation the powerful Sir Thomas More, Henry VIII's Chancellor. More erected his own private chapel and tomb in the church before his fall from power, but his remains were buried elsewhere after his execution in 1535. By the early nineteenth century it was clear that St Luke's had become too small for its community, and a new much larger parish church was built in Sydney Street in 1824 dedicated to St Luke. Shortly afterwards the early riverside church became known as Chelsea Old Church, and it remains Chelsea's oldest building today. Another building of note on the Chelsea Embankment is Crosby Moran Hall. Entirely Tudor in its appearance, it incorporates the original sixteenth-century Crosby Hall and has been lovingly restored and rebuilt over three decades to resemble a great mansion of the period along with its own Tudor garden and courtyard.

Readers will no doubt wonder why some buildings fail to appear in this book, particularly those that carry the word 'Chelsea' in their title. This is generally because they fall within the boundary of another borough, such as Chelsea Football Club which is based in the borough of Hammersmith and Fulham.

My aim in writing is to include buildings that have stories to tell, contain history and architectural merit or perhaps are associated with famous people. From spending many hours walking about the area, I believe that Chelsea is far more than a leafy London suburb; it has connections with the river, royalty, food (it was here that the Chelsea bun was first sold in the eighteenth century), artists and writers, entertainment and even a former power station that powered the London Transport network for most of the twentieth century. It is really a fascinating part of town and a great place to sit and watch the world go by.

Please note: Chelsea is not an entirely discrete area so for the purposes of this book its boundaries have been set as follows: Fulham Road to the north, the Chelsea Embankment to the south, Chelsea Harbour to the west and Chelsea Bridge Road to the east.

How to Use This Book

In accordance with the 50 Buildings series, the buildings appear in chronological order according to the time of their original construction.

The accompanying map identifies each building by a number that corresponds to the numbers used in the text.

Website information for buildings that are open to the public is provided at the end of each chapter.

Please Note

Many of the buildings within the book appear on English Heritage's Register of Listed Buildings, a designation that recognises historic and/or architectural significance. This 'listed status' (ranging from the top Grade I, through II* to II) necessitates strict planning rules which helps to prevent essential features of the buildings from being lost, preserving them for future generations.

The 50 Buildings

1. Chelsea Old Church, No. 64 Cheyne Walk, SW3

Chelsea Old Church sits beside Chelsea Embankment and is famous for its rich history and associations with royalty and the nobility. It is known from papal records that a stone church has existed on the site from at least 1290. Over the centuries chapels were added to the chancel and then a nave and tower in the seventeenth century. It was the main parish church to serve the local community before Chelsea's population grew extensively in the early 1800s.

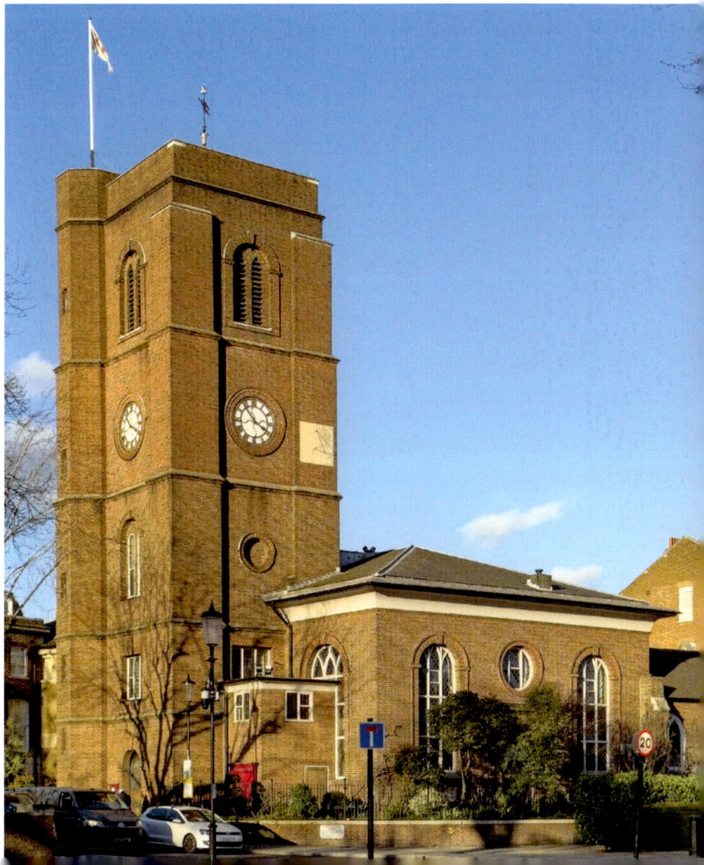

Chelsea Old Church.

Many prominent figures such as King Henry VIII, several of his wives, his Chancellor, Sir Thomas More, as well as Henry's daughter Princess Elizabeth (later Queen Elizabeth I), Lady Jane Grey, James I and the physician and naturalist Sir Hans Sloane have worshipped here. In the nineteenth century the church was included in landscapes painted by the artists James McNeill Whistler and J. M. W. Turner.

Like many eminent people of the period, Thomas More lived beside the Thames in an opulent residence. This allowed him to enjoy Chelsea's good clean air away from London's noisy and polluted streets. His house and grounds were vast, stretching inland from the river and covering much of the area we now know as Beaufort Street. A regular worshipper at Chelsea Old Church (then known as St Luke's), he rebuilt the church's southern chapel in 1528 as his own private chapel; remarkably, this still stands despite the enormous devastation caused to the church, its tombs and monuments resulting from enemy bombing in 1941.

After the war Chelsea Old Church underwent major restoration, which returned much of the building to its seventeenth-century appearance. A visit to the present church is an absolute delight. Not only picturesque with its arches, box pews and vaulted wooden ceiling, it boasts a set of chained books – unique in London's churches – and a very fine collection of church monuments, including

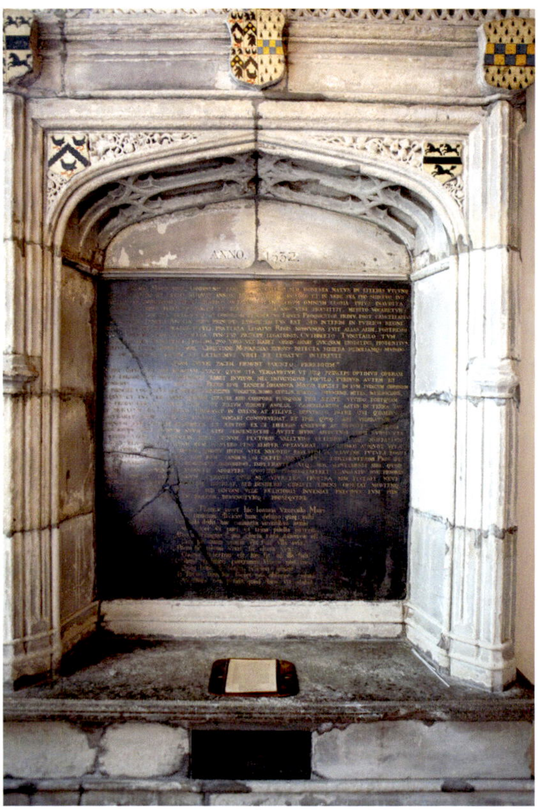

Tomb of Sir Thomas More.

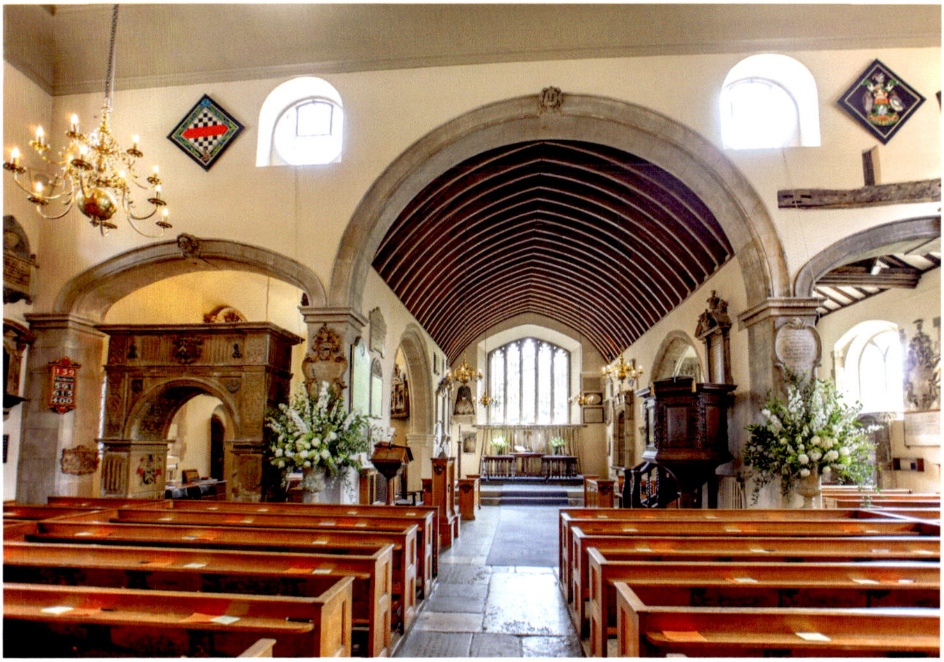

Chelsea Old Church.

one to Sir Thomas More in the Sanctuary. More's refusal to accept Henry VIII as Head of the Church of England resulted in him being given a traitor's death, and while a tomb for More exists within the church, his remains are buried elsewhere (in the Tower of London and in St Dunstan's Church, Canterbury).

www.chelseaoldchurch.org.uk

2. Crosby Moran Hall, Cheyne Walk, SW3

Just a little further west from Old Chelsea Church is a magnificent example of medieval domestic architecture, Crosby Moran Hall. Originally based in Bishopsgate in the City of London, Crosby Place (as it was then known) was built in the late fifteenth century for Sir John Crosby, an extremely affluent merchant, politician, soldier and diplomat. It was the grandest of mansions and undoubtedly reflected his wealth and status. Crosby died in 1476 after which the building was occupied by other notable luminaries including the Duke of Gloucester, later to become Richard III, and then Sir Thomas More. Unfortunately, much of the building was destroyed in a fire in 1672, leaving only the great hall and one wing standing. New owners in 1907 wanted to demolish the building, which resulted in a campaign to save it, spearheaded by the National Trust and British Archaeological Society. Having won their battle, the structure was moved piece

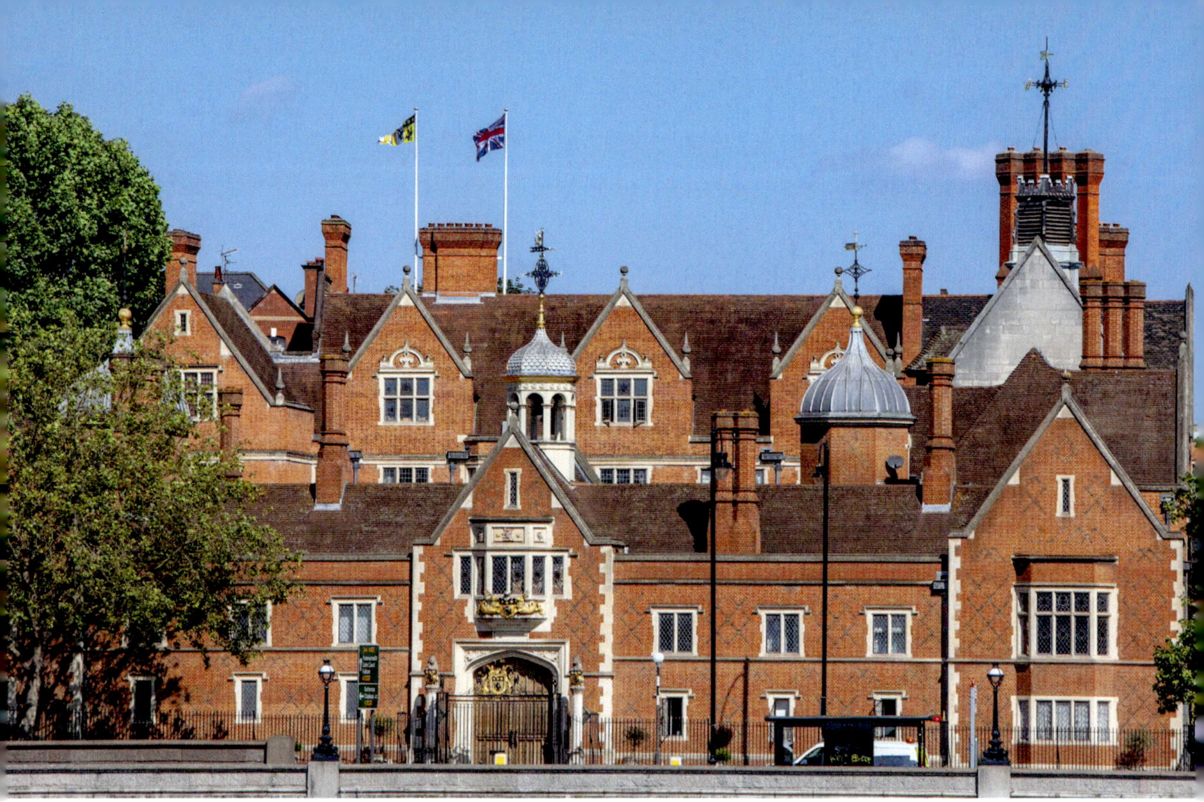

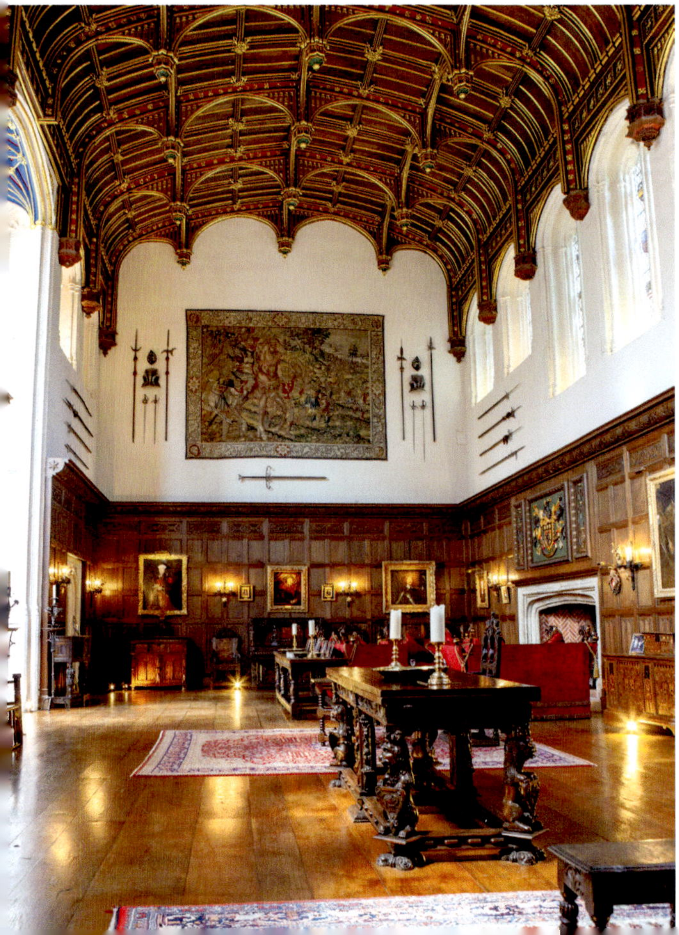

Above: Crosby Moran Hall.

Left: The great hall.

by piece to a new site on Chelsea's riverfront in 1910 (which had previously been Sir Thomas More's estate). Its relocation was overseen by the architect Walter Godfrey, who then added his own neo-Tudor brick buildings around the original great hall. In the 1920s Godfrey further installed an Arts and Crafts residential wing to the hall when the building was occupied by the British Federation of University Women.

When the Greater London Council, the hall's owners, put the building up for sale in the mid-1980s, Dr Christopher Moran, the noted businessman and president of Co-Operation Ireland, became its proud new owner. A man with an exceptional passion for architectural heritage, especially that of the Tudor period, Dr Moran has spent more than thirty years lovingly restoring the hall, fashioning it into his private home using the existing buildings and erecting new ones. He is responsible for creating an entirely new Tudor estate, the work of highly skilled heritage craftsmen using the construction methods of the sixteenth century. Filled with opulent furnishings, marvellous ceilings, paintings, decorative devices and emblems, the palatial home also has a magnificent chapel that has been ecumenically blessed, and a Tudor garden filled with plants solely from the period. Crosby Moran Hall is indeed a tribute to the Tudor era and is utterly unique within central London today.

www.christophermoran.org

The chapel.

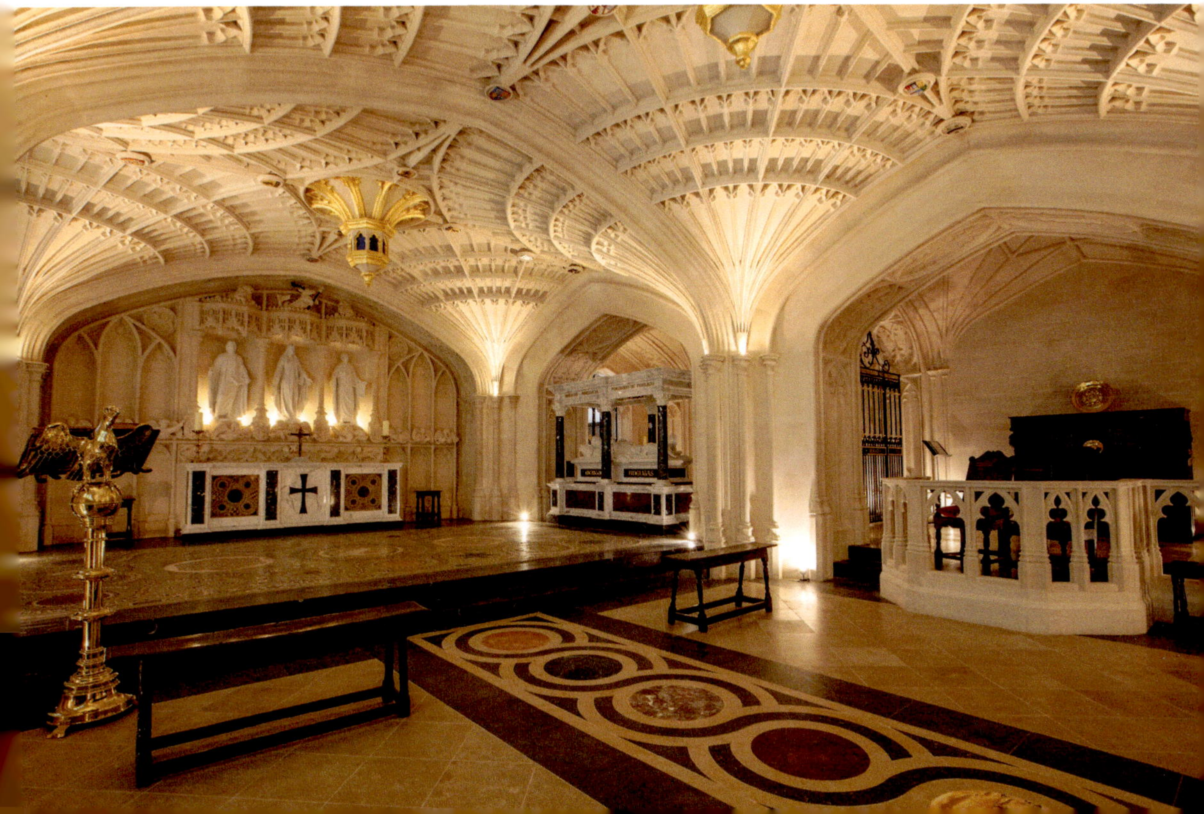

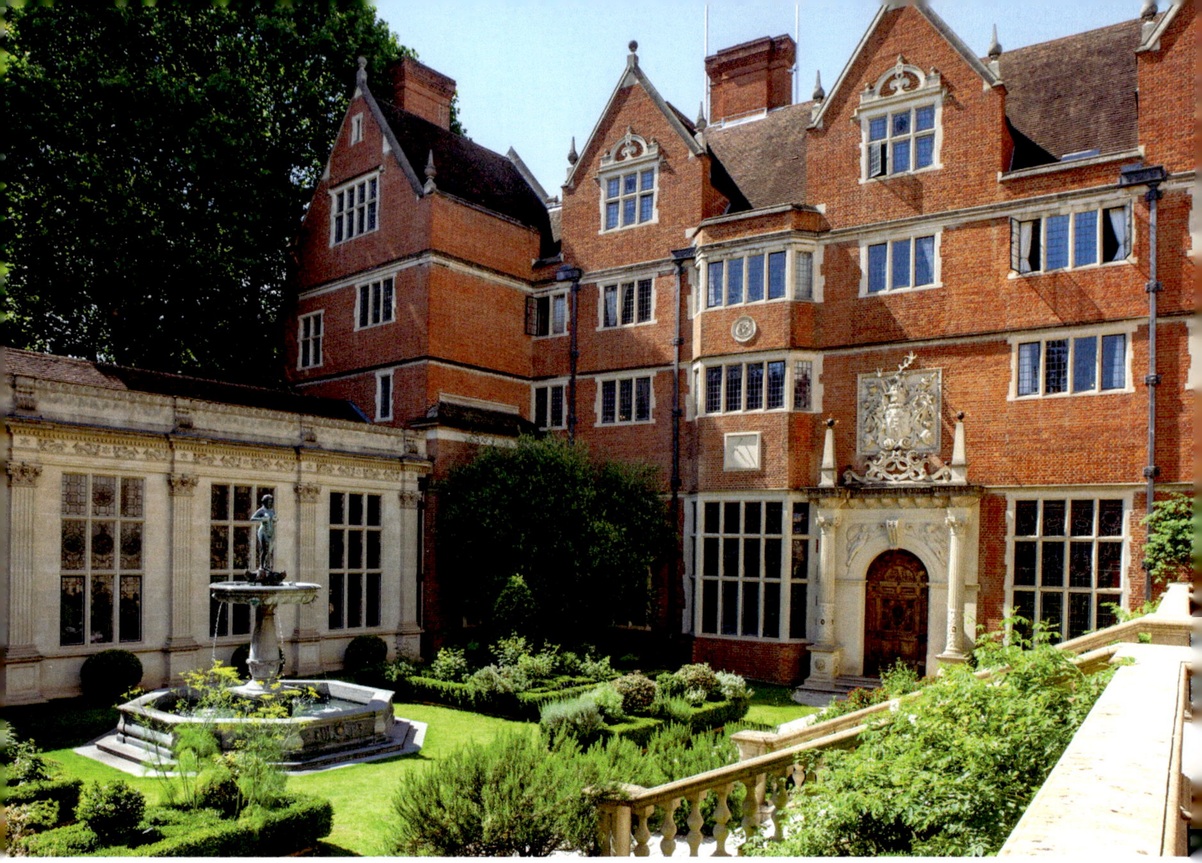

The courtyard.

3. Chelsea Physic Garden, No. 66 Royal Hospital Road, SW3

The land on which Chelsea Physic Garden sits was originally leased to the Worshipful Company of Apothecaries in 1673 and covered an area of approximately 4 acres with a river frontage on the Thames. The company established a medicinal garden on the land which was to be used as a place to train the apothecary apprentices. At this time the role of apothecaries was largely to help prevent disease and to assist in healing (in keeping with a doctor's role nowadays). By the early eighteenth century the garden was in financial difficulties, but due to the actions of Sir Hans Sloane, Chelsea's lord of the manor, the Apothecaries' 'Physic' garden, was rescued. In 1722 Sloane granted the company a new lease on the site on the condition that it paid a yearly £5 fee, a condition that it still complies with today.

By building a tall brick wall around the physic garden a microclimate was formed and this made it possible for exotic plants, herbs and a great variety of trees to be grown in the grounds. The garden still has walls on three of its sides and although nothing remains of its original seventeenth-century glasshouse the garden's listed Victorian glasshouses have just been lovingly restored and are now once again open to the public. After the Apothecaries relinquished ownership of the garden in the

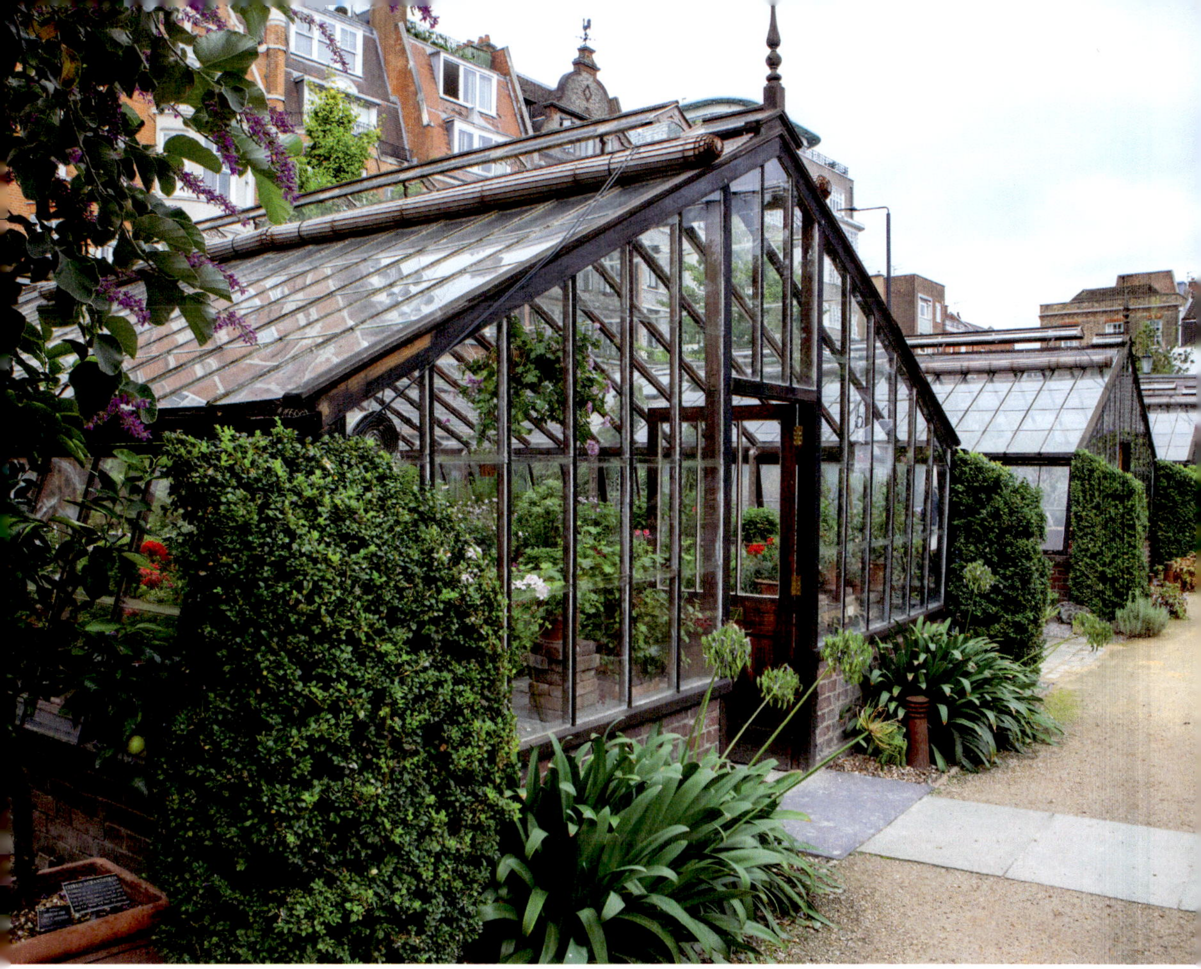

Greenhouses, Chelsea Physic Garden.

1890s the London Parochial Charities took over its care. Since the 1980s the garden has been owned and managed by the Chelsea Physic Garden Company and is now a very popular attraction attracting visitors from across the globe.

www.chelseaphysicgarden.co.uk

4. Lindsey House, Nos 95–101 Cheyne Walk, SW3

Located close to Battersea Bridge, Lindsey House is believed to be the oldest house in the borough and is regarded as being one of Chelsea's old 'palaces'. The original house, built on the site of Sir Thomas More's garden, was rebuilt in 1674 as the magnificent family home of Robert, Earl of Lindsey, Lord Great Chamberlain to Charles II, and immediately became known as Lindsey House.

About 100 years later Count Zinzendorf, a philanthropist and aristocratic leader of the Protestant Moravian sect purchased the house for use as its headquarters, hoping to transform the building into a settlement for his

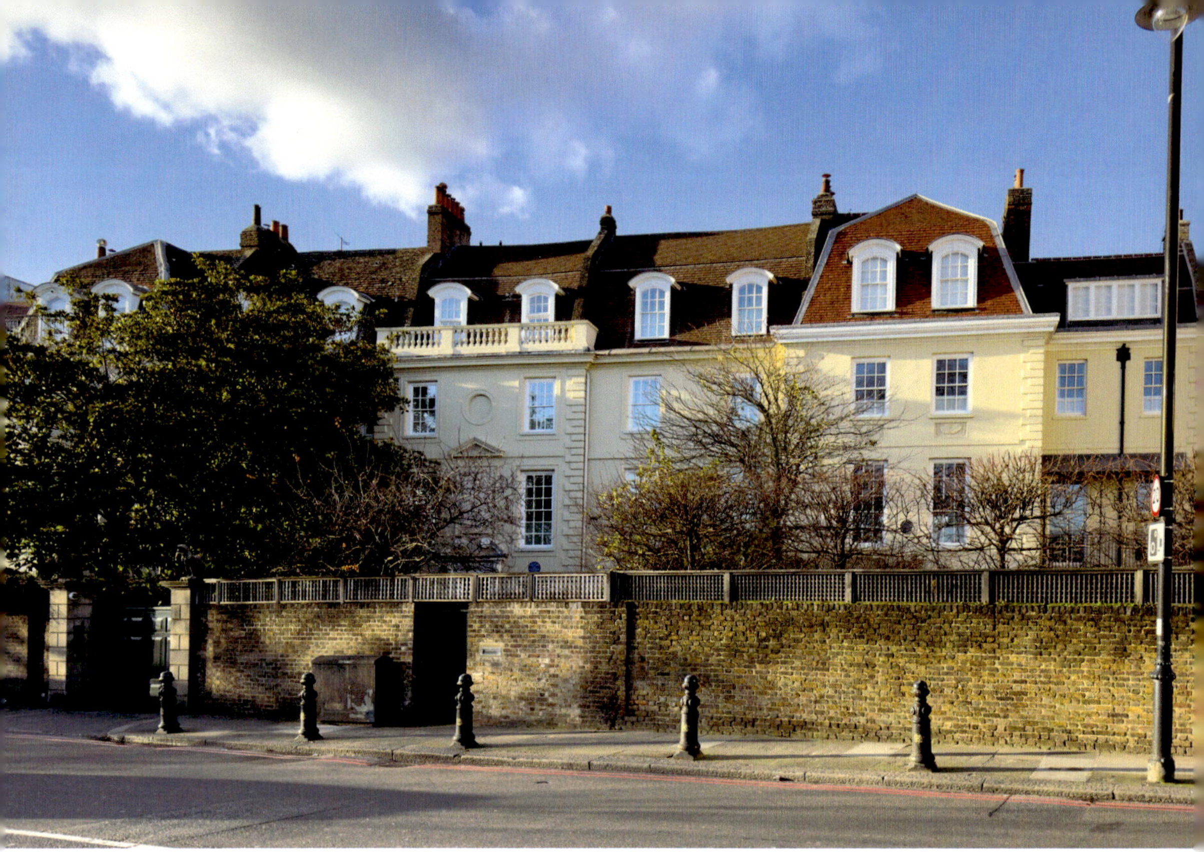

Lindsey House.

brethren. Zinzendorf began renovating the building, but his plans for a sizeable colony were never materialised. After his death in 1760 the property was once again sold, and the Moravians left. All that remains today to remind us of this period is their chapel, manse and burial ground, built on the Lindsey House estate just behind the King's Road. Following its sale in the 1770s the substantial house was rearranged and split into individual homes, which nowadays stretch between Nos 95 and 101 Cheyne Walk. Despite many external and internal alterations, the houses still retain many beautiful features including a Grade II listed garden behind Nos 99–100 that was created by Sir Edwin Lutyens and Gertrude Jekyll.

Since being divided up Lindsey House has been home to a number of famous people. In the early 1800s the father and son engineers Marc and Isambard Kingdom Brunel lived at No 98, while the celebrated American painter James McNeill Whistler occupied No 96 from 1866 until 1878. In the early twentieth century the Irish art collector and founder of the Dublin Picture Gallery, Sir Hugh Lane, was a tenant at Nos 99–100 (now a single house). It was under his residency that the house was restored and the garden redesigned. He tragically died as a passenger on the British ocean liner *Lusitania* when it sank in 1915 after a German U-boat attack. Two of the houses are today owned by the National Trust.

5. The Royal Hospital Chelsea, Royal Hospital Road, SW3

Constructed between 1682 and 1692, the magnificent Royal Hospital was an entirely novel institution in Britain and purportedly modelled on Louis XIV's recently erected Hotel des Invalides in Paris. It was set up by King Charles II to provide a home for wounded soldiers and the aged who had returned home injured after serving overseas and were now deemed unfit for duty. The king created Britain's first standing army after his restoration to the throne and felt the country had a debt of duty to look after its veterans who would otherwise be without access to welfare, medical care and housing. The creation of a Royal Hospital, in reality a care home, would not only ensure the wellbeing of his soldiers but it would also be a valuable institution and a lasting memorial to the king's reign. The hospital finally opened in 1692 with a complement of 476 male residents who became known as Chelsea Pensioners.

The building, designed by the celebrated architect Sir Christopher Wren (renowned for his work on St Paul's Cathedral), consisted of three quadrangles, an impressive colonnade, a chapel and great hall. Accommodation for each of the pensioners was a 6-foot square 'berth', situated on 'long wards' in ranges facing the quadrangles. In recent times the sleeping quarters have been greatly enlarged and each pensioner's room now has a study area and en suite facilities. An infirmary was also built by Wren, a place to treat any injured or sick pensioner. This was rebuilt in the early 1800s and again in 2009 when it was renamed The Margaret Thatcher Infirmary, after Britain's first female prime minister. Today it functions both as a medical centre and hospice.

After the hospital opened its extensive grounds were transformed into Ranelagh Gardens, which became one of London's most popular pleasure gardens during the

The Royal Hospital Chelsea.

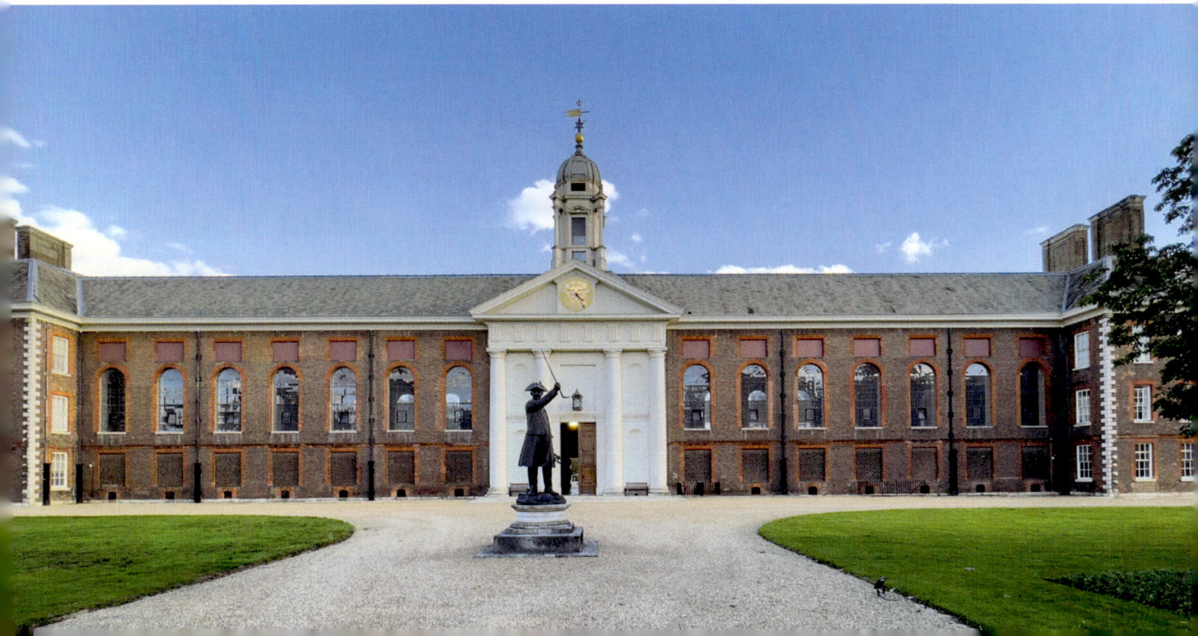

eighteenth century. Nowadays this is where the internationally acclaimed RHS Chelsea Flower Show is held each May. It is easy to spot the Chelsea Pensioners (both men and women today) by their colourful blue or red uniforms; they are great ambassadors and provide regular tours of the Royal Hospital, which can be booked online.

www.chelsea-pensioners.co.uk

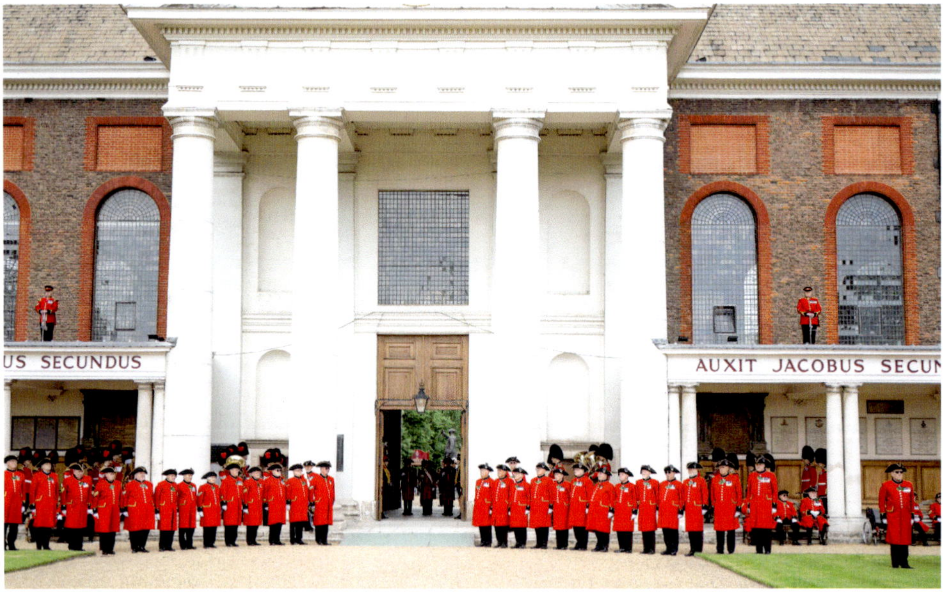

Above: The Royal Hospital Chelsea. (Courtesy Royal Hospital Chelsea, © Peter Kindersley)

Below: The Royal Hospital Chelsea. (Courtesy Royal Hospital Chelsea)

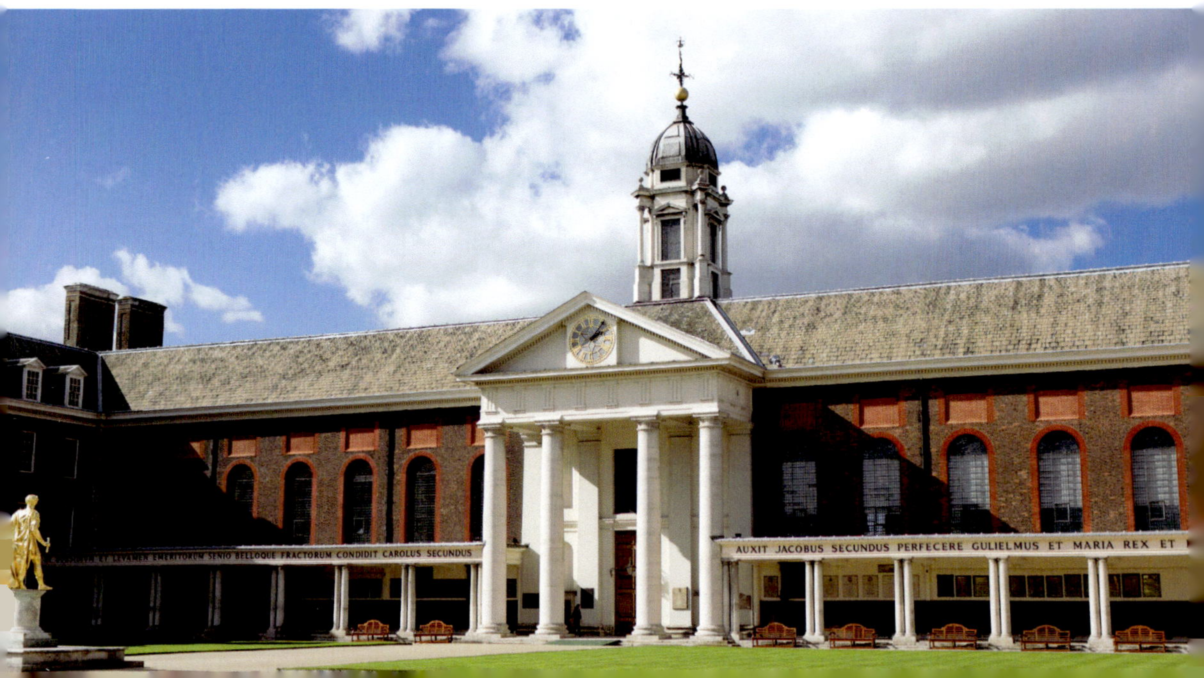

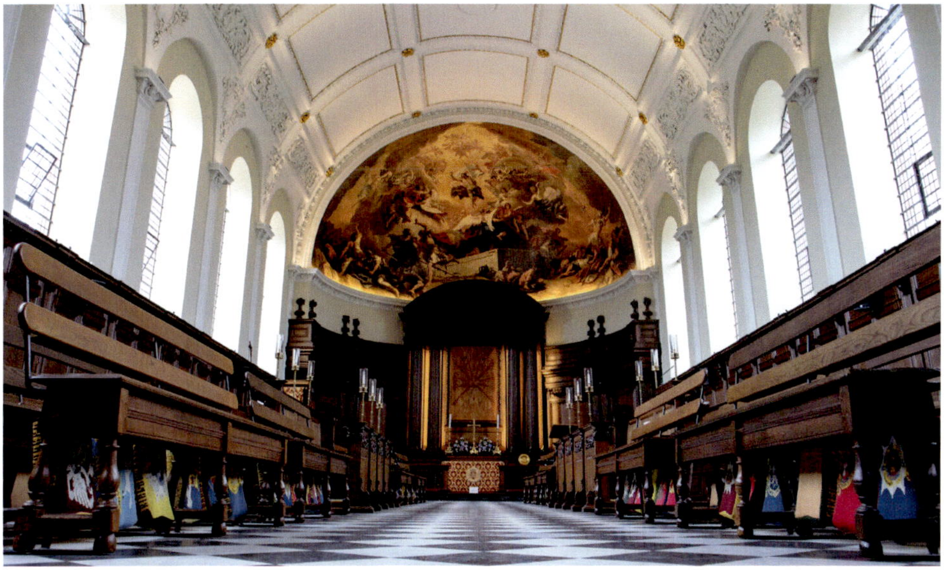

The chapel. (Courtesy Royal Hospital Chelsea)

6. Royal Avenue, Chelsea, SW3

Standing on the King's Road at its junction with Royal Avenue presents the visitor with possibly one of Chelsea's most impressive views. For it is from here that one sees Wren's masterpiece, the Royal Hospital Chelsea, in its majesty. Its imposing main entrance dominates the landscape and Royal Avenue acts like a foyer to the splendid building.

Royal Avenue.

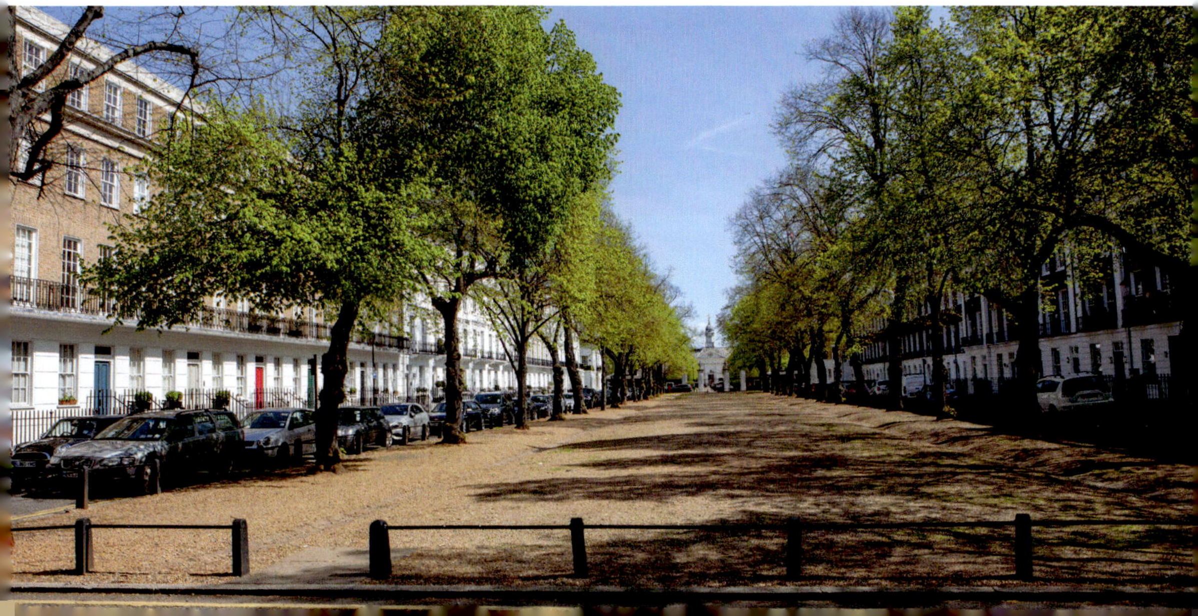

Built in the late 1600s Royal Avenue was apparently intended to be part of a longer grand route between the Royal Hospital and Kensington Palace, but this never materialised. In many respects the name 'Royal Avenue' is a misnomer as it not an avenue but resembles a long narrow square with terraced housing on two sides. The houses date to the early to mid-nineteenth century and many today carry a Grade II listing. The central area between the houses is filled with gravel, and tall plane and lime trees line the avenue.

At its southern end Royal Avenue meets St Leonard's Terrace, where the author Bram Stoker lived when writing his famous work *Dracula*. Royal Avenue's beautiful setting has also attracted notable residents including the singer Petula Clark, the architect Richard Rogers and the film director Joseph Losey, and is mooted to be the home of Ian Fleming's fictional character James Bond.

7. Riverside Pubs: The Cross Keys and No. Fifty Cheyne, SW3

Until the Chelsea Embankment was constructed in 1874, the waters of the River Thames gently lapped against Chelsea's riverside buildings. The river was still a major means of transport, and customers may well have arrived at the riverside pubs by boat. After the Great Stink of 1858 when London was plagued by noxious smells and raw sewage in the Thames, the river was narrowed and embankments with underground sewers were created by Sir Joseph Bazelgette, designed to take away London's waste. Though highly successful the new embankments resulted in the relocation inland of the pubs and taverns that had previously lined the river.

The Cross Keys.

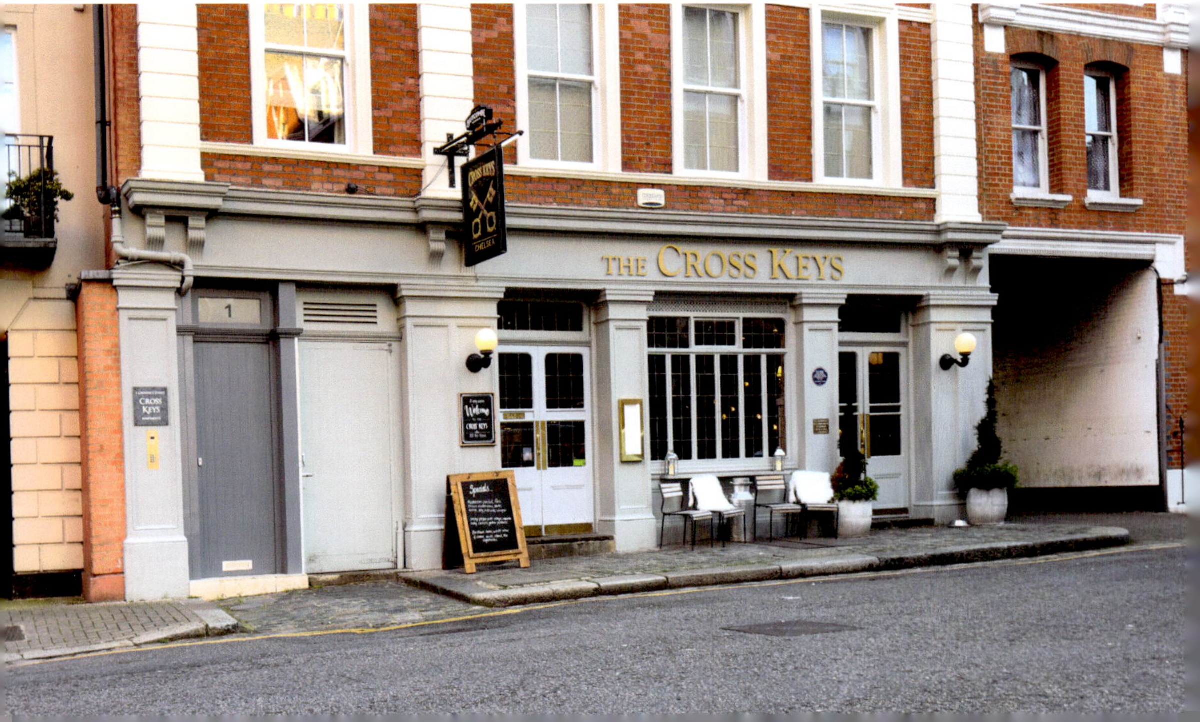

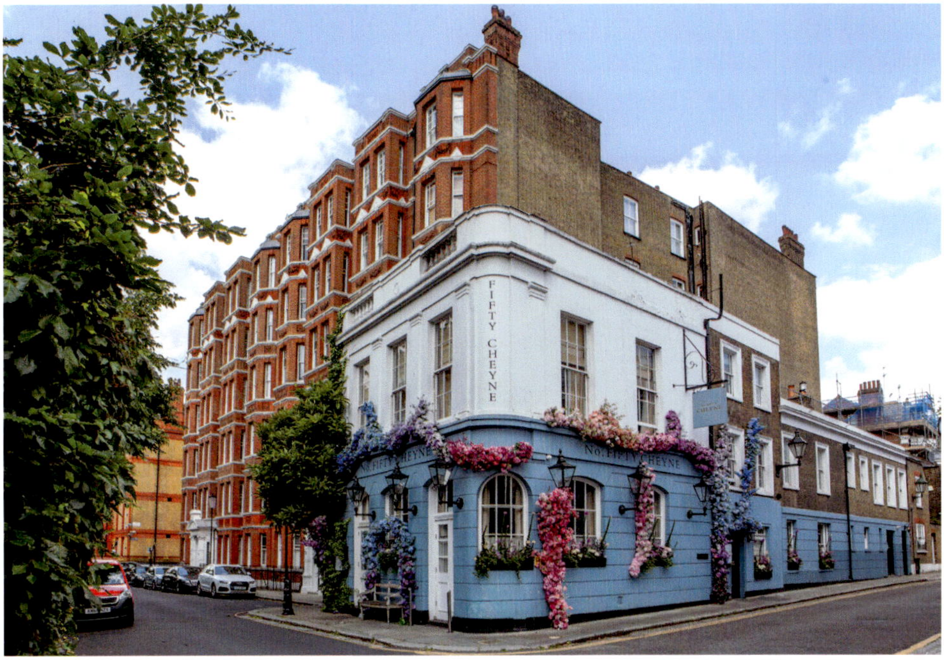

No. 50 Cheyne.

An excellent example of this is the 1708 Cross Keys pub at No. 1 Lawrence Street. Thought to be Chelsea's oldest pub, images exist showing its original position beside the water, but you will have to cross the busy Chelsea Embankment to drink there today. The pub, always extremely popular, is renowned for its celebrity clientele including names such as Bob Marley and Agatha Christie and the artists Turner, Whistler and Sargent.

Nearby, No. 50 Cheyne Walk was also once a riverside tavern. Built in the early 1800s, it was known as The King's Head and Eight Bells and was a popular haunt of Dylan Thomas in the 1940s. Nowadays, it is a restaurant known as No. Fifty Cheyne and offers patrons wonderfully curated dishes of the highest quality in a most comfortable and elegant setting.

www.butcombe.com/the-cross-keys-pub-chelsea
www.fiftycheyne.com

8. Carlyle's House, No. 24 Cheyne Row, SW3

This brown-brick terraced house was erected in 1708 at a time when Chelsea was far from the fashionable enclave it is today. From 1834 it was home to the famous Scottish writer, historian and social observer Thomas Carlyle (1795–1881) and his wife Jane. The house, typical of the period, is part of a row of similar-looking houses.

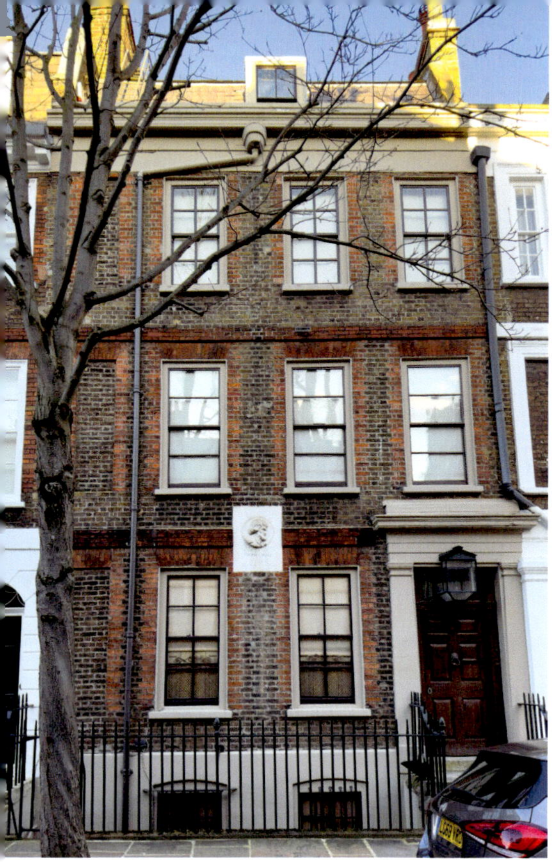

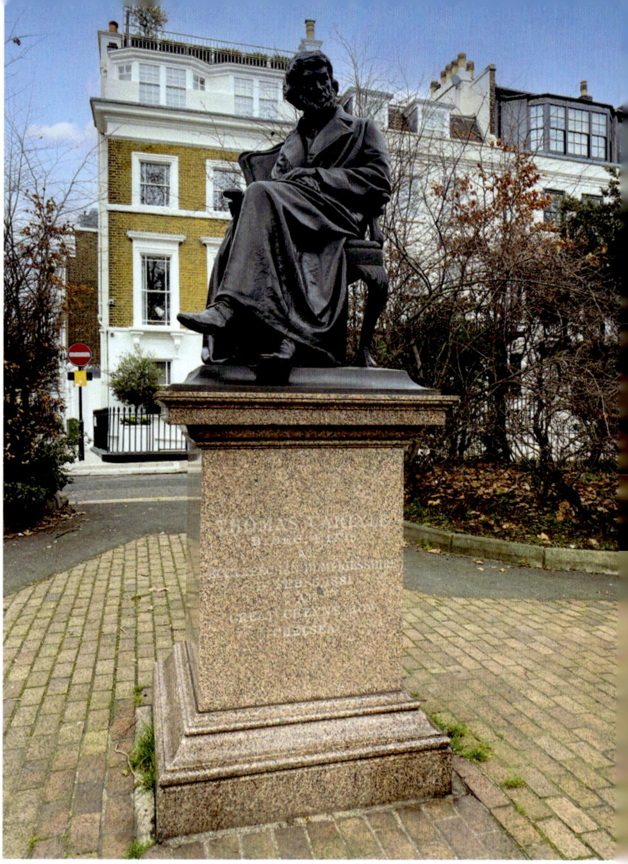

Above left: Carlyle's House.

Above right: Carlyle's statue, Chelsea Embankment Gardens.

It holds a Grade II* listing and has a commemorative wall plaque on the façade containing a medallion portrait of Carlyle. Three storeys high and with a basement, the house also boasts a soundproofed attic that Carlyle had specially built and used as his study, a place where he could work in peace and drown out the noise of the street.

Carlyle, affectionately known as 'The Sage of Chelsea', was not only a historian and writer but also a very great social observer who in the Victorian period exerted a strong influence on its society. He was rated a literary genius by his contemporaries who flocked to Cheyne Row to spend time in his company. The house was always full of members of the intelligentsia, academics, artists, writers and forward-thinkers of the day like Dickens, Browning, Darwin, Tennyson, Mill and Ruskin. His wife Jane was equally literary minded and an acclaimed letter writer. She was as popular as her husband and reputedly a wonderful host.

In 1837 Carlyle published his celebrated epic history *The French Revolution*, a work consisting of three volumes. Having completed the first volume, he lent it to his friend John Stuart Mill to critique. Not realising the manuscript's importance Mill's maid mistakenly destroyed it and used it to light the fire! Despite this catastrophic setback Carlyle completed volumes II and III and then rewrote the first volume from scratch.

Since 1895 the house containing Thomas and Jane's possessions, their paintings, furniture, books and letters has been open to the public. Nowadays it is owned and managed by the National Trust and opens between Easter and October. Well worth a visit, the museum is most atmospheric and contains original fixtures and fittings as well as wallpaper by William Morris.

www.nationaltrust.org.uk/visit/london/carlyles-house

9. Argyll House, Nos 211–17 King's Road, SW3

Architecturally and historically significant, No. 211 King's Road, also known as Argyll House, was designed to be a private family home by the Venetian architect Giacomo Leoni and built in 1723. It is a marvellous example of Leoni's Palladian architectural style and manages to combine façades boasting Italian Venetian features such as the stone doorcase with Doric columns, along with English domestic floor plans – both reasons for its Grade II* English Heritage listing. Despite its position on the busy King's Road, the house attracted the cream of London's society in the early 1900s. Here the occupants, the renowned interior decorator Lady Sybil Colefax and her husband Sir Arthur Colefax, an MP and patent lawyer, hosted lavish parties to A-list celebrities that included the

Argyll House.

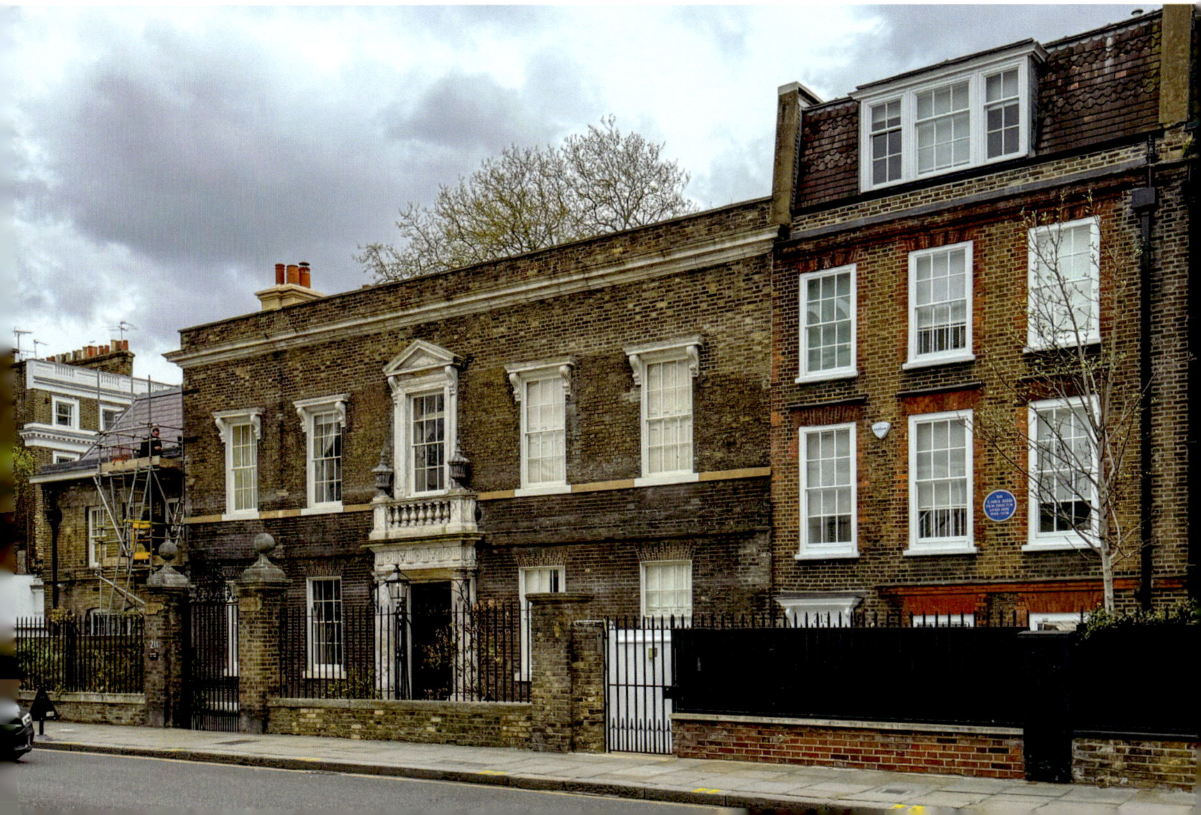

Churchills, Noel Coward, Fred Astaire, Virginia Woolf, as well as Edward VII and Wallis Simpson. In fact, it is alleged that Wallis and Ernest Simpson met the future king here in 1935. Many of the Colefaxs' guests were also Sybil's clients due to the success of her interior design company, Sybil Colefax Ltd (later Colefax & Fowler), which she had launched after the couple had lost much of their fortune in the Wall Street Crash.

Living right next door at No 213 was another society hostess, Syrie Maugham. She was not only famous for being married to the author, Somerset Maugham, but also for being the daughter of Dr Barnardo who founded the children's charity, and as the former wife of the American pharmaceutical giant, Henry Wellcome. An interior designer like her neighbour Sybil, she introduced the so-called 'Vogue Regency' style, a new fashion that embraced all-white interiors. Her own drawing room decorated in all shades of white became instantly popular and was a fashion immediately adopted by high society. She too was a much-admired hostess and regularly entertained artists, nobility, the 'in' crowd and the literati in her home. Later between 1948 and 1978 the film director Carol Reed occupied the house.

No 215 King's Road is also renowned; the composer Dr Thomas Arne resided here in 1771, while the actress Dame Ellen Terry, lived here between 1904 and 1920.

10. Duke of York Square, Royal Military Asylum and the Saatchi Gallery, SW3

Today people watching is possibly the most common pastime for anyone visiting Duke of York Square as it is a superb traffic-free space that boasts numerous cafés, restaurants and shops as well as commercial and residential accommodation. It is the ideal place to meet friends and business colleagues and generally watch the world go by. This new square, built on the grounds of the former Royal Military Asylum, was the brainchild of the Cadogan Estate and designed by the architects Paul Davis + Partners. Since it opened in 2003 it has become a major feature of the area, attracting both independent and high street stores. It even has its own luxury family-run store and delicatessen, Partridges, which serves members of the royal family and bears a royal warrant on its façade.

The new Duke of York Square sits beside the impressive 1803 Royal Military Asylum. The idea for such an institution was put forward at the end of the 1700s following the deaths of so many servicemen in the Napoleonic Wars, and it was built to educate and provide boarding for 1,000 orphan children (700 boys and 300 girls) of regular soldiers. The school's pupils wore distinctive uniforms: red jackets, blue breeches and black stockings for the boys and red gowns, blue petticoats and white aprons for the girls. As was common in the period the girls were trained in domestic tasks and duties whilst the boys not only learned to read and write but were also prepared for work in one of several trades. When the school moved out of its premises in the early 1900s the building then became the London headquarters of the Territorial Army until 2003. Since 2007 the Saatchi

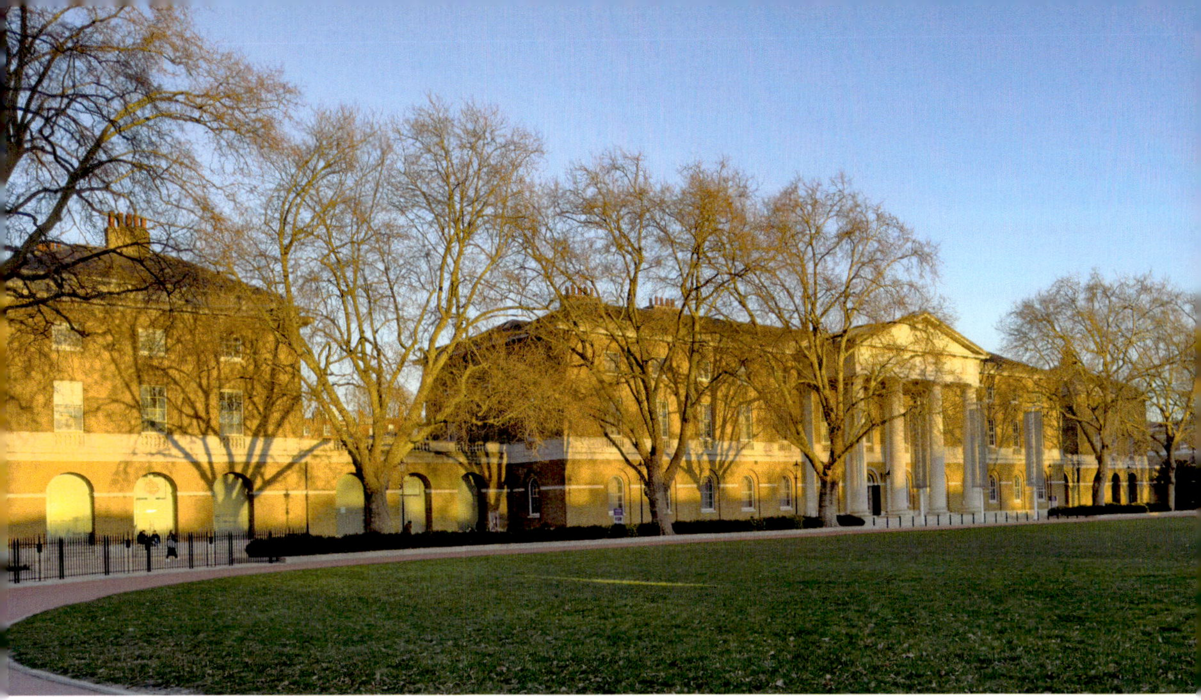

Above: The Saatchi Gallery.

Below: Duke of York Square.

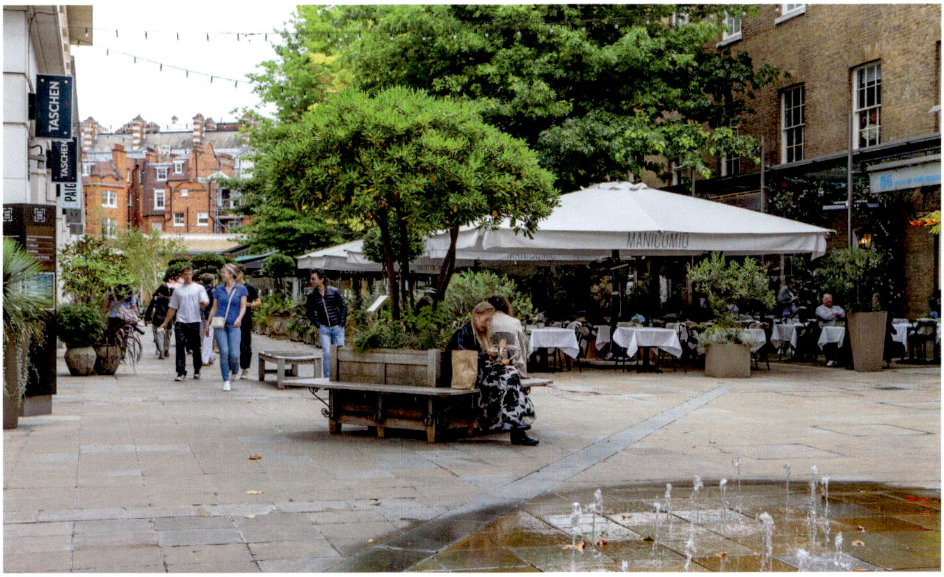

Gallery has occupied the main building and has contributed much to Chelsea's cultural scene. Displaying contemporary art across fifteen well-proportioned exhibition spaces, the gallery aims to show works of today – those that might not be seen in other institutions. Charles Saatchi's first London gallery opened in 1985 and since that time his mission has been to support the work of emerging artists and to make contemporary art accessible to all.

11. Cheyne Walk, SW3

Certainly one of London's most stylish and desirable addresses, Cheyne Walk runs both east and west of the Albert Bridge and has been home to nobility and the rich and famous for centuries. Many of the grand houses originally had a direct entrance on to the Thames, but when the Chelsea Embankment was built this changed and their properties became separated from the riverside. Although Henry VIII's magnificent manor house dominated this stretch of the river in the Tudor period, it was demolished in the mid-1700s after the death of its then owner, Sir Hans Sloane.

Perhaps the best-known houses of the street are Nos 4–18, located at Cheyne Walk's eastern end. No. 16, Queen's House, is the largest and most impressive and was where the artist Dante Gabriel Rossetti lived with his brother William and

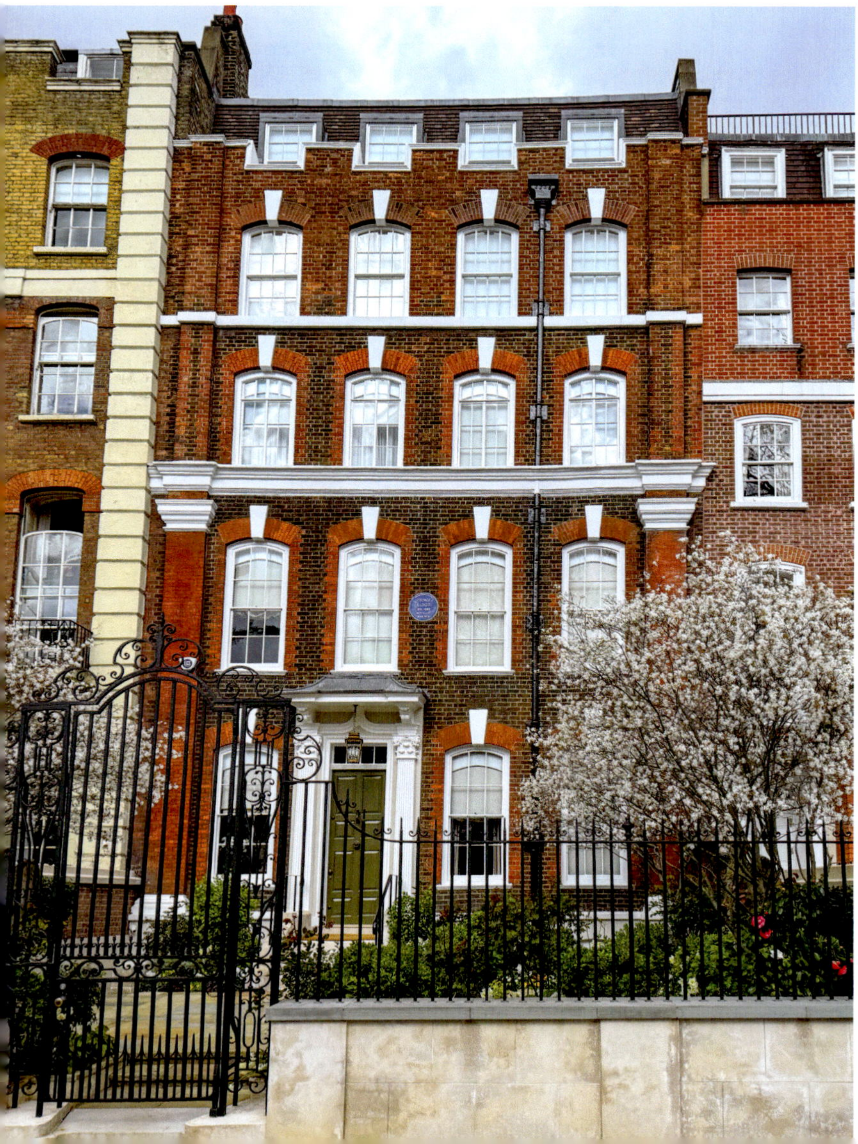

George Eliot's house.

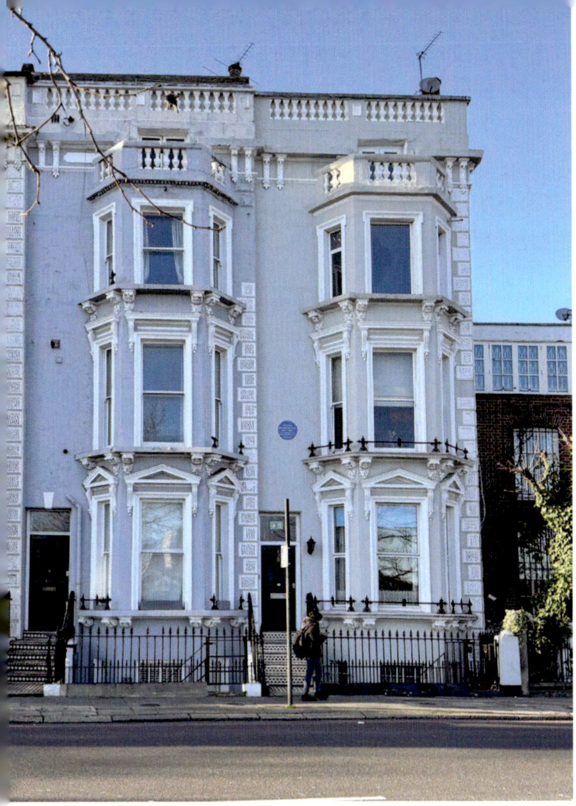

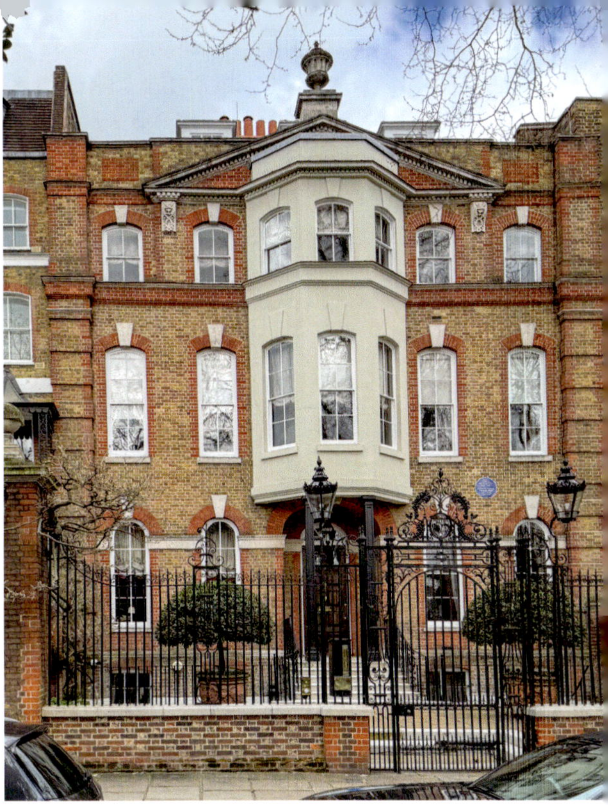

Above left: Sylvia Pankhurst's house.

Above right: Rossetti's house.

the poet Algernon Swinburne. A beautiful early eighteenth-century Queen Anne townhouse, it became the main hub in the 1860s for the Pre-Raphaelite artists and their muses. Rossetti's house was renowned not only for its stream of literary and artistic visitors but also for its exotic and unusual garden menagerie, which included a wombat, kangaroo, armadillo and several noisy peacocks.

Other famous names to have lived here include the composer Arthur Sullivan, writer George Eliot, the former twentieth-century prime minister David Lloyd George and composer Ralph Vaughan Williams. Recent residents include the cartoonist Gerald Scarfe and his wife, actress Jane Asher, and the American businessman and politician Michael Bloomberg.

Walking along the street westwards you encounter a host of English Heritage blue plaques that commemorate noted personalities such as Hilaire Belloc, Walter Greaves, Sylvia Pankhurst, John Tweed and Mrs Gaskell. Others who have lived here include Mick Jagger and Ronnie Wood of the Rolling Stones, novelist and politician Ken and Barbara Follett, the artist J. M. W. Turner and Russian businessman Roman Abramovich.

Surprisingly, a children's hospital was established on Cheyne Walk in the latter part of the nineteenth century. Although its beautiful 1888 building still stands at Nos 60–61 it now contains luxury apartments. The hospital moved out in 1993 and became part of the Chelsea and Westminster Hospital.

12. King's Road Boutiques: Mary Quant and Vivienne Westwood

Built in the late 1600s as the private road of the monarch Charles II and stretching from London to Kew and Hampton Court, the King's Road was given public status in 1830 and today functions as Chelsea's main high street. It is filled with upmarket designer boutiques, independent fashion shops and high street stores, and buzzes with activity. People from every walk of life shop here and the area is a true mecca for fashionistas. Reflecting the character of the district the shops are particularly stylish and often expensive, but if you're looking for something unique then the King's Road is undoubtedly the place to shop.

Nowadays the road has the appearance of gentility, but not so very long ago this was not the case. From the mid-twentieth century it had a reputation for being a bohemian centre, a place to pick up outrageous clothing and to be seen. It was on the corner of Markham Square and the King's Road that the fashion designer Mary Quant opened her boutique Bazaar in 1955. Here she created an entirely new look for women and promoted seemingly revolutionary styles such as the miniskirt, hot pants, trousers and high boots – undoubtedly avant-garde for the

Location of Mary Quant's boutique, Bazaar.

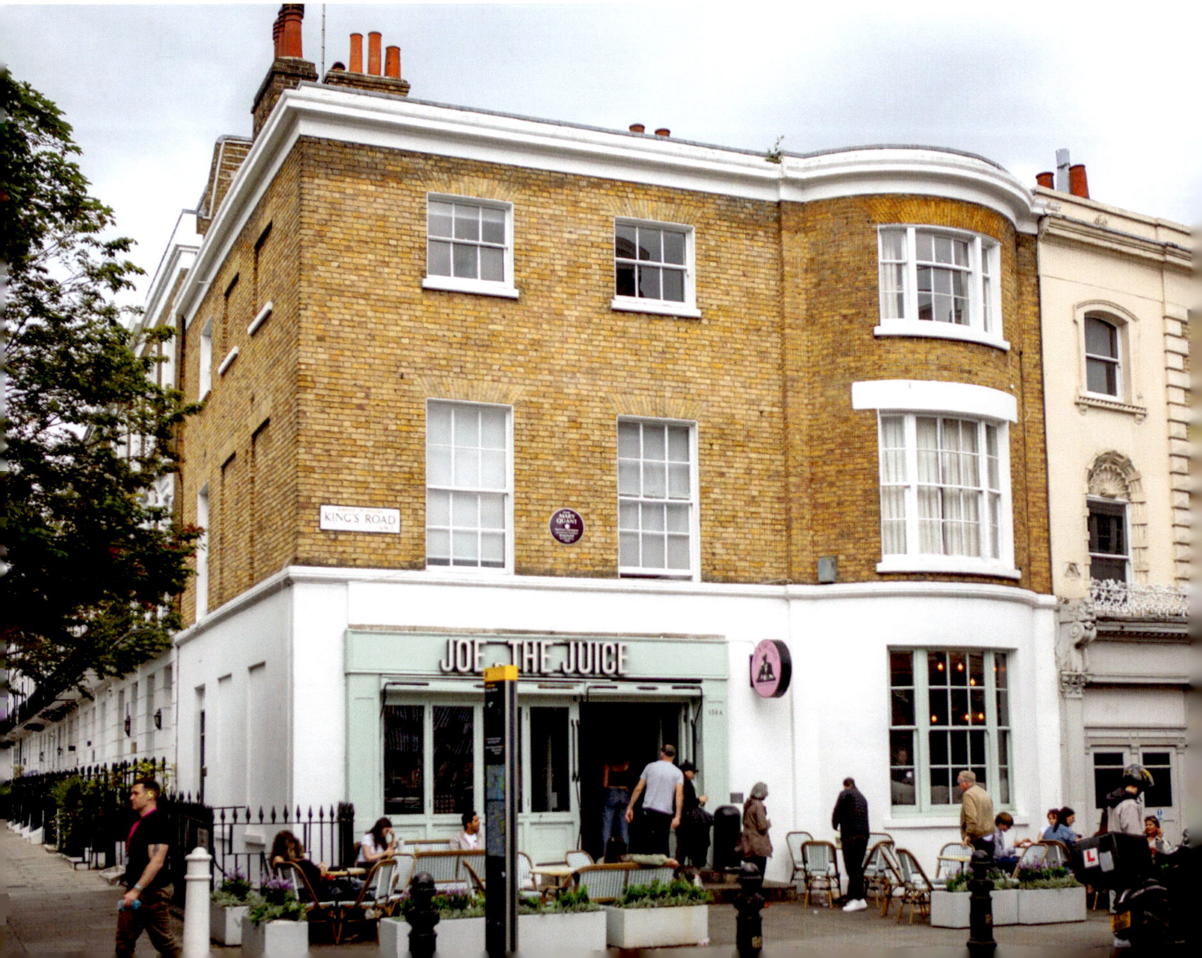

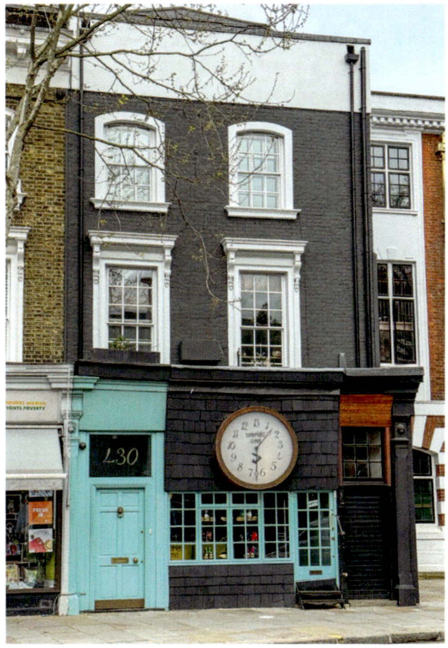

Vivienne Westwood's boutique.

time. Her fashions were a massive success and extremely popular with teenagers and youngsters who could be seen mincing along the King's Road at all times of the day and night. In the era of female emancipation Quant's designs and clothing resonated with an entire generation of young women, allowing them, possibly for the first time, to acknowledge their own individuality.

By the 1960s music and fashion were firmly ensconced along the street, with rockstars, musicians and celebrities frequenting its many colourful boutiques, but when in the early 1970s Vivienne Westwood opened Let it Rock at the World's End it caused a sensation. Its name changed frequently, as did the clothing, which became increasingly unorthodox in style. Malcolm McLaren, Westwood's husband, was jointly running the shop whilst managing the punk band the Sex Pistols, so the shop's merchandise included much punk paraphernalia including safety pins, chains and latex outfits.

Although these times have long since passed, the King's Road is still one of London's main fashion hubs.

13. St Luke's and Christchurch, Sydney Street, SW3

St Luke's Church sits on a prominent site just behind the King's Road on Sydney Street. It is a truly magnificent building in the late Gothic style and well deserving of its Grade I listed status. With its pronounced flying buttresses and tower topped with pinnacles the church is naturally a local landmark. It was built in the early 1820s to meet the needs of the rapidly increasing population and replaced (and

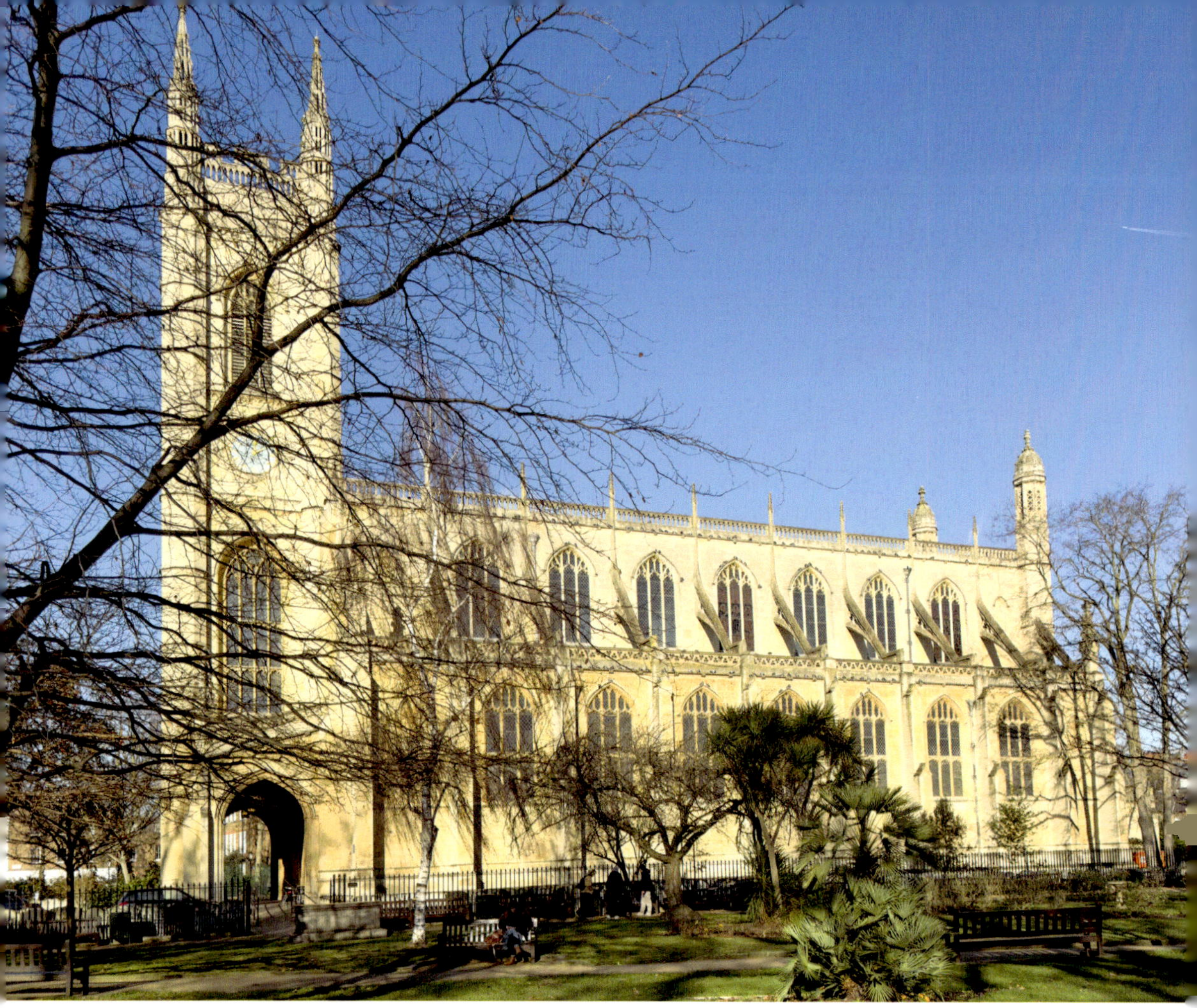

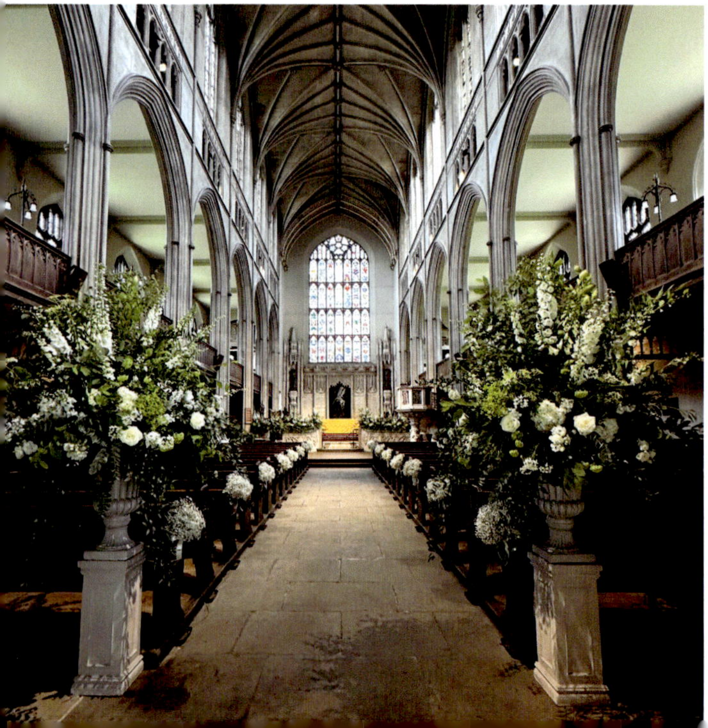

Above and left: St Luke's and Christchurch.

took the name of) the former medieval parish church, today's Chelsea Old Church, located on the banks of the Thames. St Luke's is the work of James Savage, an expert on medieval architecture who won a competition for its design. He produced not only one of the earliest neo-Gothic churches constructed in London at the time, but also the tallest nave (60 feet high) of its parish churches. The church is constructed of Bath stone and architectural historians have expressed its similarities with King's College Chapel Cambridge, and Bath Abbey.

St Luke's has a vast interior and was originally laid out in the style of a preaching house with a huge pulpit, upper galleries, tiny altar and many pews. This changed later in the century when it underwent alterations resulting in its present appearance. Of particular interest is Hugh Easton's post-war east window which contains exquisite stained glass full of vivid colours and the emblems of saints.

It was in the church on 2 April 1836 that Charles Dickens married Catherine Hogarth just a couple of days after the publication of the first part of his *Pickwick Papers*. Other famous names associated with St Luke's include the parents of the founder of the Scouting Movement: Robert Baden-Powell, who was married here in 1846, and Sir John Goss, who wrote the hymn, 'Praise My Soul, the King of Heaven'. Interestingly, the first rector of the church was Revd Hon. Gerald Valerian Wellesley, who was both the husband of Lady Cadogan and brother of the Duke of Wellington. The Cadogan family have always been major patrons of St Luke's, and many memorials commemorate them in the church. Since 1986 St Luke's and Christ Church have united to form a single parish.

www.chelseaparish.org

14. Godfrey Street and Chelsea Green, SW3

Moments away from the noise and bustle of the King's Road, it is hard to believe that Godfrey Street, with its brightly coloured terraced housing and air of tranquillity, is so close by. It is almost like walking into another world and it is certainly an unexpected treat. The street is a delightful enclave and feels homogenous, even though the houses are not identical and display a substantial blend of architecture. Since they were built around 200 years ago many have been altered, but that does not detract from their appeal, and today they are highly sought after and no longer house the working classes for whom they were built.

At the north end of Godfrey Street you find Chelsea Green, the sole surviving part of old Chelsea Common, which is a great favourite with local residents. A wonderful mix of independent shops, cafés and restaurants here attract a loyal clientele and include all the essential businesses you would expect around a village green, such as a fishmonger, butcher, baker, greengrocer and delicatessen. There is also a wine merchant, cheesemonger, pharmacy, florist and children's clothing shop. Chelsea Green itself is a small, landscaped area offering seating and a fountain amongst greenery.

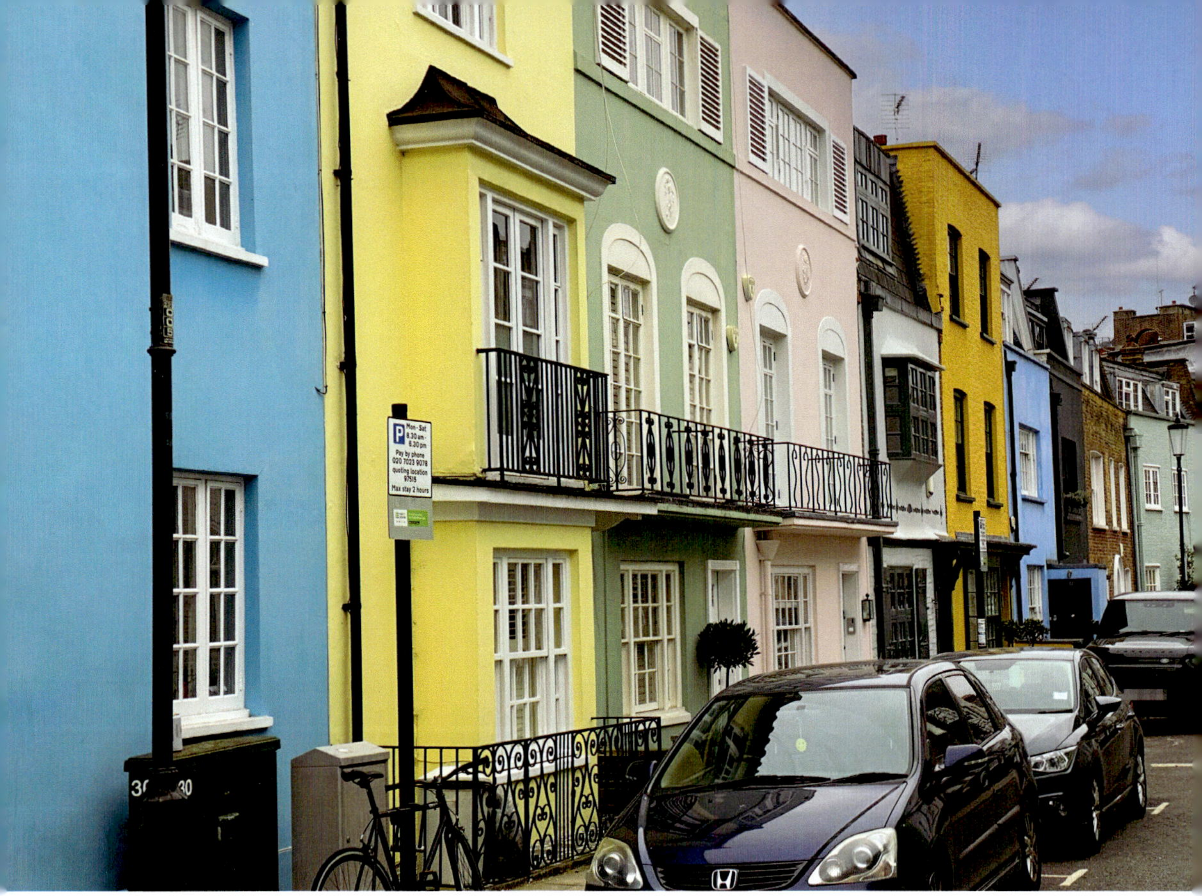

Above: Godfrey Street.

Below: Chelsea Green.

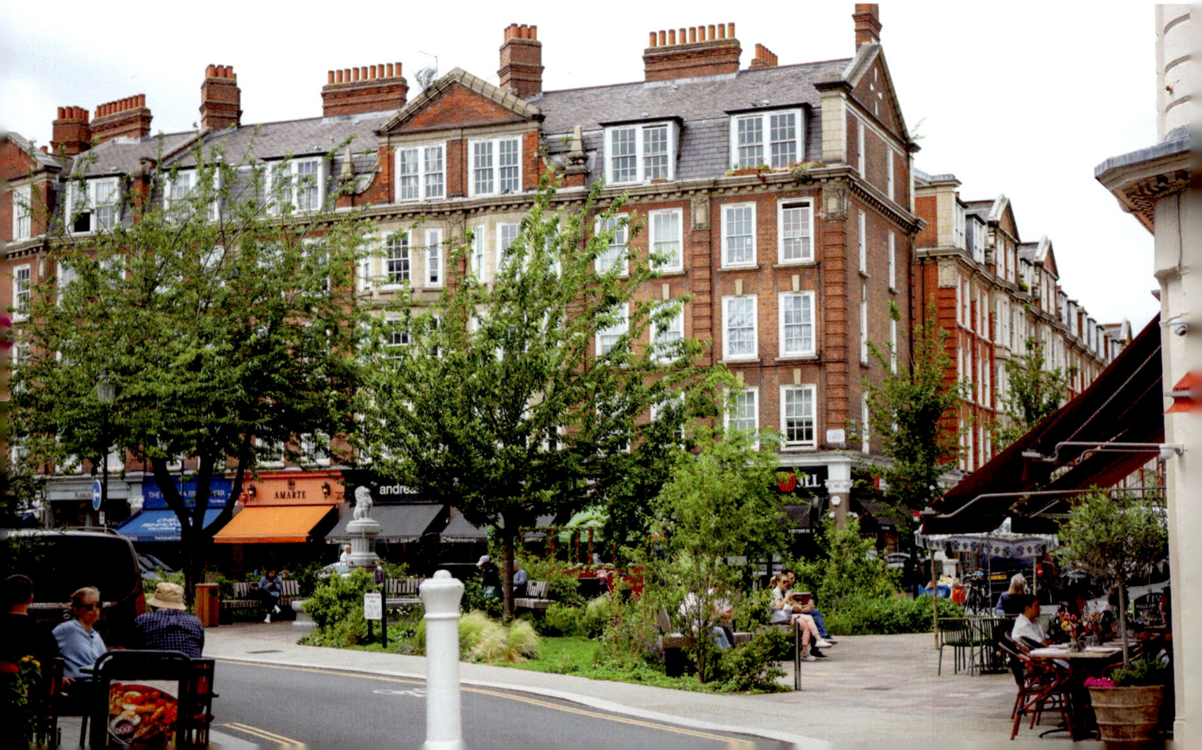

15. Chelsea Potter Pub, No. 119 King's Road, SW3

Easily spotted for its colourful display of hanging baskets and the pub's prominent sign depicting a man holding a pot, the Chelsea Potter sits at the junction of Radnor Walk and the King's Road. The pub belongs to Greene King and is known for its wide variety of beers, wines, spirits and cocktails. It is a sports bar and serves classic pub food and Sunday roasts. The building itself dates to 1842 and is typically Victorian in style with wooden floors, interior columns and etched-glass windows.

When it opened it was known as the Commercial Tavern and remained as such until 1958 when its name changed to the Chelsea Potter. Why this came about is a little unclear; maybe it was due to the proximity of the Chelsea Pottery studio along the street at Nos 13–15 Radnor Walk established by David Rawnsley in 1952 (later run by Brian Hubbard). This was an open studio for potters and had a celebrity following, including members of the Rolling Stones, Jimmy Hendrix and Paul McCartney, who were also customers of the pub. However, this pottery was not the first to come to Chelsea as William de Morgan, the innovative designer of the Arts and Crafts movement and great friend of William Morris, had set up and

Chelsea Potter.

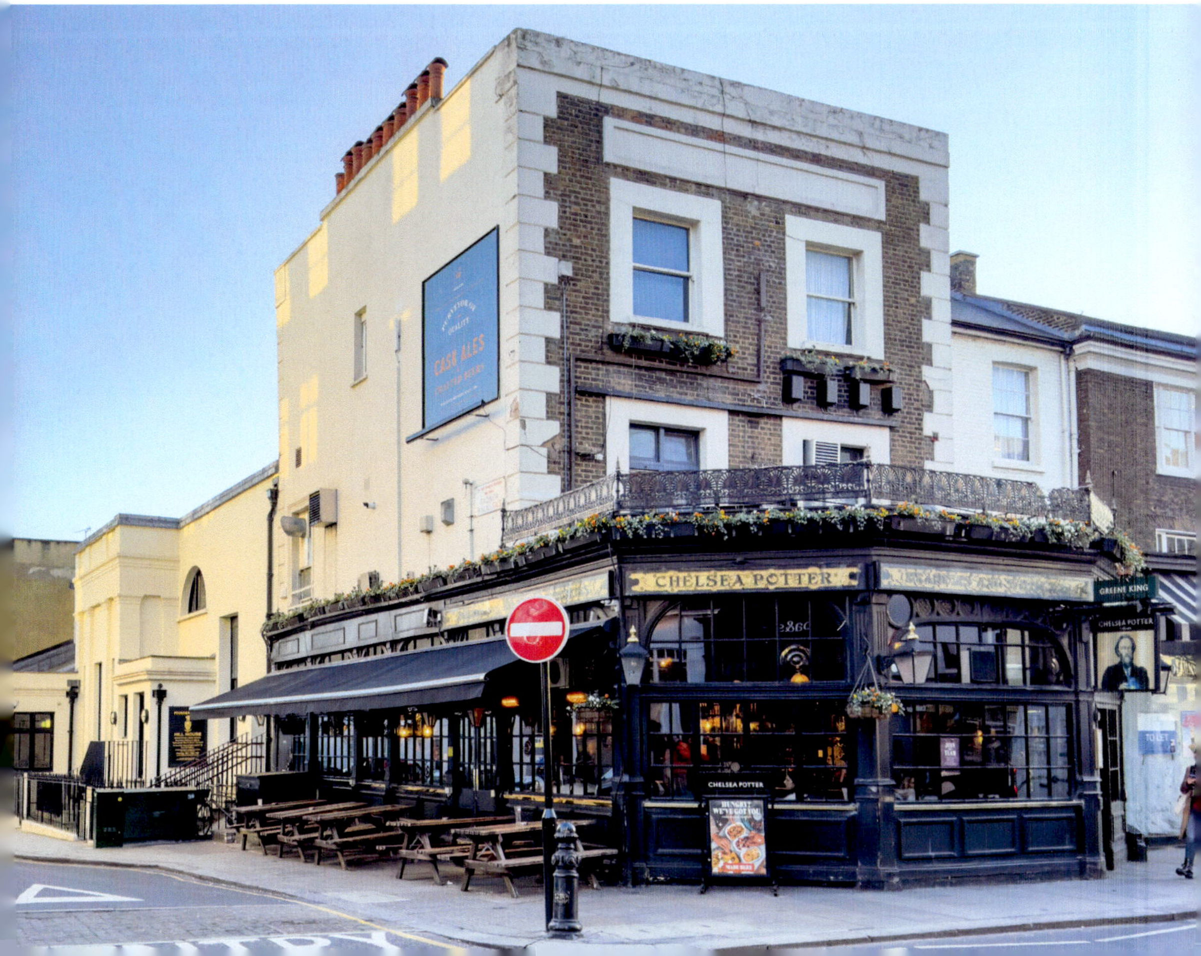

run his famous Chelsea Pottery almost 100 years earlier on Cheyne Row. It seems unlikely, however, that the pub would have adopted its new name to recognise de Morgan as his business had ceased trading in 1907. Maybe the change in name simply remembers the impact of pottery on the locale as there had been a Chelsea porcelain factory here in the mid-1700s whose products were coveted by the rich and famous of the day. Whatever the reason both William de Morgan and his wife Evelyn are greatly associated with Chelsea and with the set of artists who lived and worked here in the mid- to late nineteenth century.

Today outstanding pieces of Chelsea porcelain and many examples of de Morgan's highly decorative ceramic tiles, vases and dishes are displayed in the V&A Museum in South Kensington.

www.greeneking.co.uk/pubs/greater-london/chelsea-potter

16. Chelsea Hospitals, Sydney Street and the Fulham Road, SW3

The Brompton and Royal Marsden hospitals were set up in the mid-nineteenth century and have established themselves as major centres of excellence throughout the world. Today, they are at the very forefront of new pioneering treatments which improve the extent and quality of people's lives.

Brompton and National Heart and Chest Hospital.

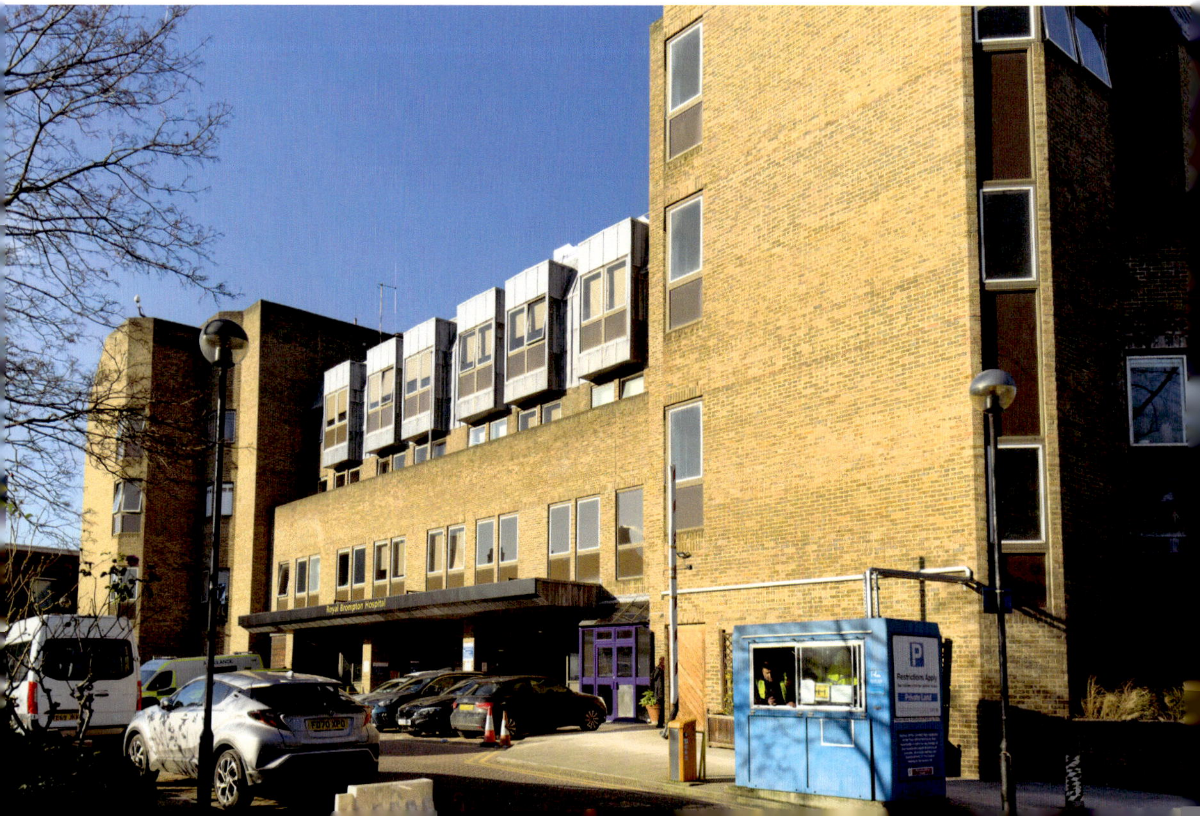

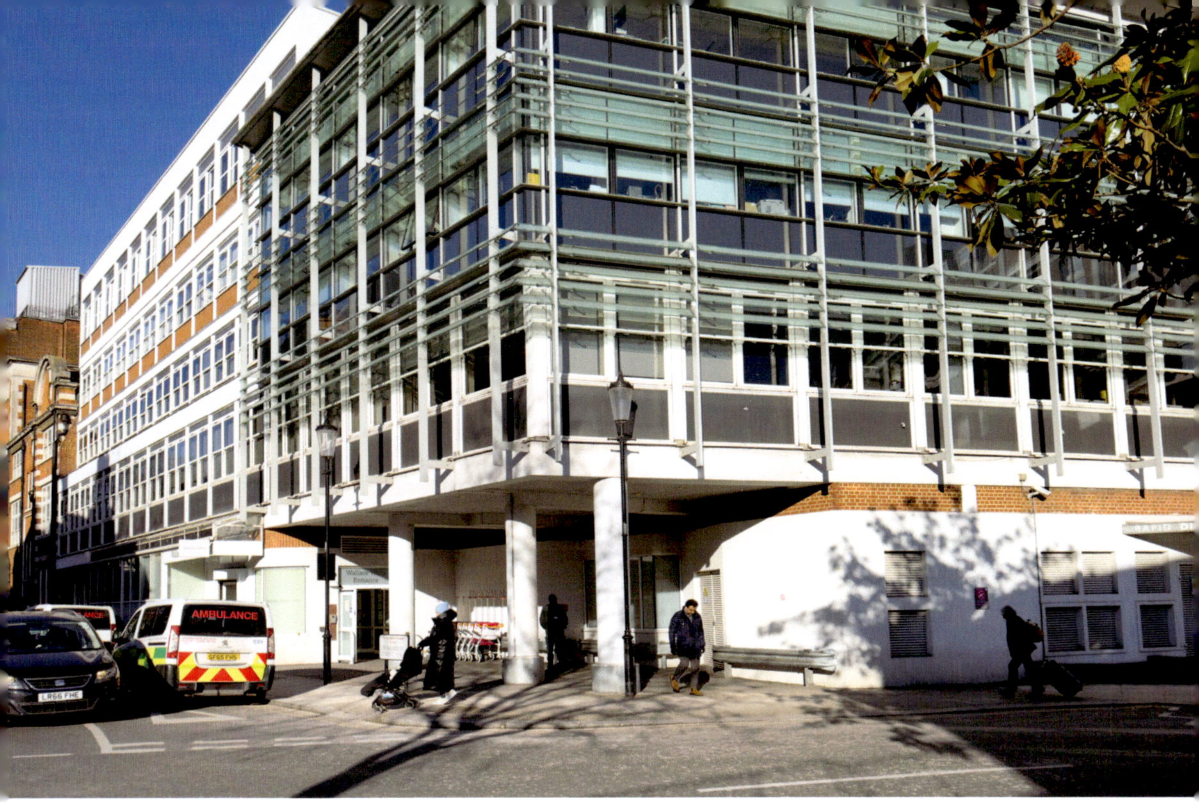

Above: The Royal Marsden, Wallace Wing.

Right: Brompton and National Heart and Chest Hospital.

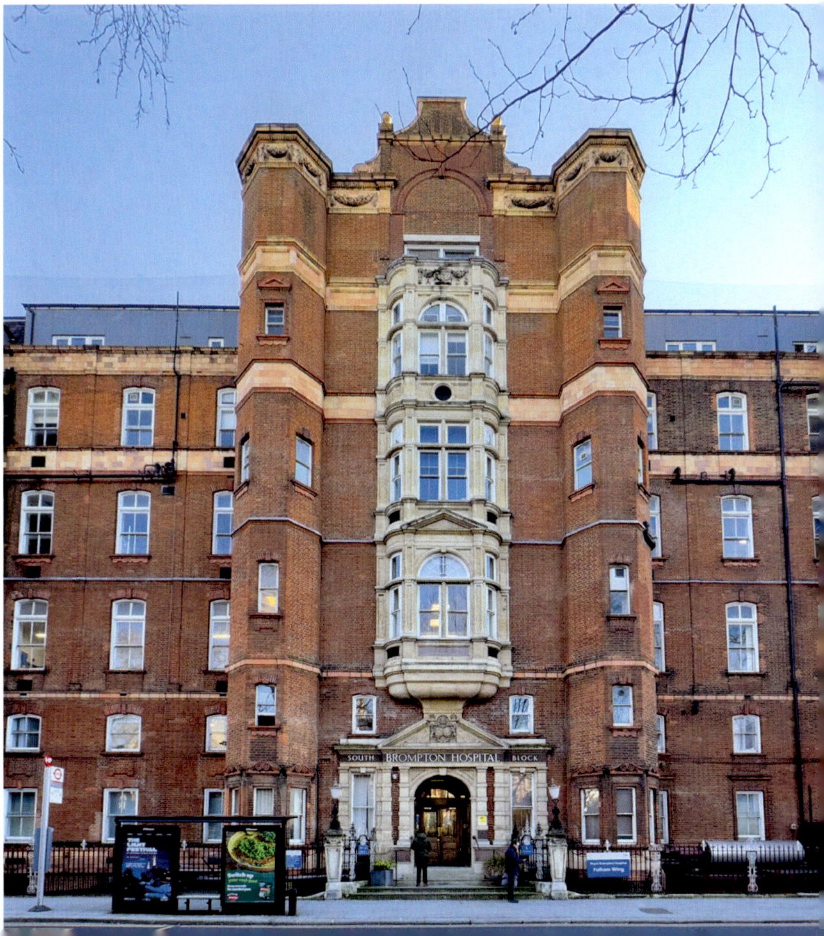

The Brompton Hospital was founded in the 1840s by solicitor Philip Rose, who was distraught to see that one of his employees stricken with tuberculosis (TB) was unable to access treatment in any one of London's general hospitals due to the infectious nature of the disease. To improve the situation, he decided to set up a specialist hospital to treat TB and other diseases of the chest. The original building situated on the north side of the Fulham Road was an imposing red-brick and black diaper Tudor-style building but was replaced in the 1980s by a new hospital in Sydney Street facing St Luke's Church. This building today, known as the Brompton and National Heart and Chest Hospital, has a strikingly long brick façade, which contrasts greatly with the red-brick blocks and the Georgian brick and stucco terraced housing in the surrounding streets. The hospital continues to lead the way both in the UK and in Europe in the treatment of and research into cystic fibrosis and of heart failure.

The Royal Marsden Hospital, based around the Fulham Road, specialises in cancer and was the world's very first hospital to be dedicated to its study and treatment. It too owes its opening in 1862 to one man, Dr William Marsden, who forty years earlier set up a non-paying hospital, the Royal Free, that provided hospital treatment to the poor. It is alleged that the effect of his wife's death from cancer was the impetus for him to found the hospital and his desire to understand more about its causes and to discover treatments for the disease. Today the Royal Marsden works alongside the Institute of Cancer Research and is internationally acclaimed for its groundbreaking research and implementation of new cancer treatments and technologies.

The Chelsea and Westminster Hospital on the Fulham Road is a teaching hospital and part of Imperial College London.

17. The Pheasantry, No. 152 King's Road, SW3

Standing out amongst its neighbours for its arched entranceway adorned with caryatids, a pair of large eagles and a quadriga, it is a surprise to discover that this stunning townhouse is nowadays home to a Pizza Express restaurant as well as a music venue.

Known as the Pheasantry, the building has an interesting history. It was first built in the late eighteenth century, although the current structure is about 100 years younger. In the 1760s it was rented to Samuel Baker, who supplied pheasants to royalty and the gentry. Baker's business lasted less than fifteen years, but the name 'Pheasantry' stuck and was retained even when the building was demolished and replaced in the late 1800s. The new owners, the Jouberts, were French craftsmen who specialised in cabinetmaking, upholstery, gilding and decoration (it is still possible to see their name and trades on the walls in the courtyard), and appreciated the somewhat grand chateau-like building, which was unusual for the area at the time. The Jouberts are still remembered today as Felix, the last member of the family

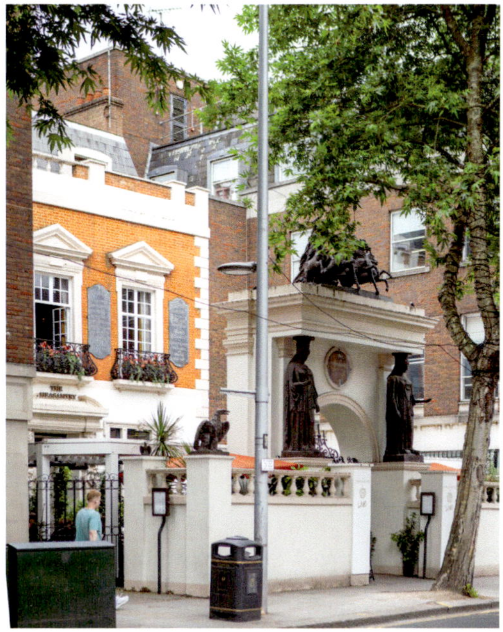

The Pheasantry.

to live here, was responsible for creating some of the miniature furniture on display in Queen Mary's dolls' house at Windsor Castle.

Shortly after the dawn of the twentieth century a section of the building was taken over by a ballet academy run by the Russian Princess Seraphine Astafieva (1876–1934), who trained the celebrated dancers Anton Dolin and Dames Alicia Markova and Margot Fonteyn. The downstairs cellar was later turned into a members-only club and gained great popularity with Chelsea's literati as well as politicians, film stars and other celebrities. Lucien Freud, Aneurin Bevan, Gregory Peck, Dylan Thomas, Augustus John and Pietro Annigoni frequented the club until it finally closed in the late 1960s. During the 1970s the Pheasantry was where musicians such as Hawkwind, Lou Reed and Queen played their early gigs and impresarios Andrew Lloyd-Webber and Tim Rice discovered the singer Yvonne Elliman. The basement continues to host daily live music performances, ranging from jazz to folk music, and retains a loyal clientele.

www.pizzaexpresslive.com

18. Glebe Place, SW3

Glebe Place is one of Chelsea's most interesting streets. It meanders south from the King's Road to Cheyne Row and is divided into segments with a dogleg in its middle section. As you enter the street from the King's Road there is a very fine long brick terrace of imposing Victorian houses, four to five storeys high. The row contrasts greatly with the buildings it faces, most of which are purpose-built artists' studios that date to the mid- to late 1800s. The Turner Studios directly opposite are purported to be where the artist J. M. W. Turner worked, but the legitimacy of this is questionable due to building's age – it was erected around thirty years after Turner's death. Further up the street at Nos 60–61 are another set of studios, Glebe Studios, which became the workplace of the artists William Rothenstein, Walter Sickert and Ernest Shepherd. Other artists to have had studios here include Charles Rennie Mackintosh, Augustus John and Winifred Nicholson.

The street has always held great appeal, possibly for its position between the river and the King's Road but also for its association with creativity. Writers such as John Galsworthy and Mervyn Peake both lived here as did Baroness Shirley Willliams, Vera Brittain, Francis Bacon and Paul Robeson.

Two houses of note are Nos 35 and 50. The former was built between 1868 and 1871 for the artist George Pryce Boyce by Philip Webb, the Pre-Raphaelite architect who had designed the Red House for William Morris. Built in red brick, No. 35 was one of the early buildings in Chelsea to display the features that later came to be known as the 'Queen Anne Revival' architectural style. With its white woodwork, tile-hung gables and chimneys the house is unmissable and clearly stands out from its neighbouring properties.

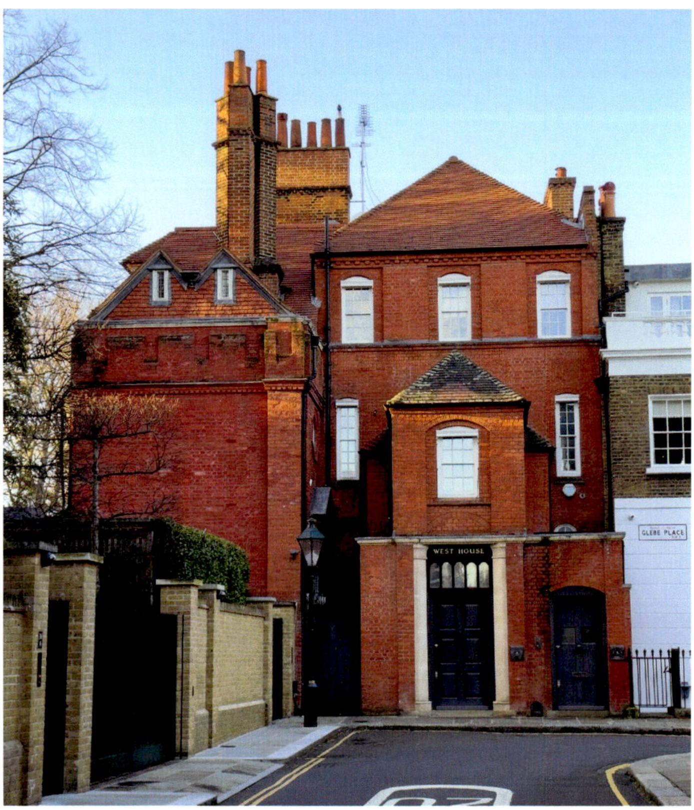

No. 35 Glebe Place.

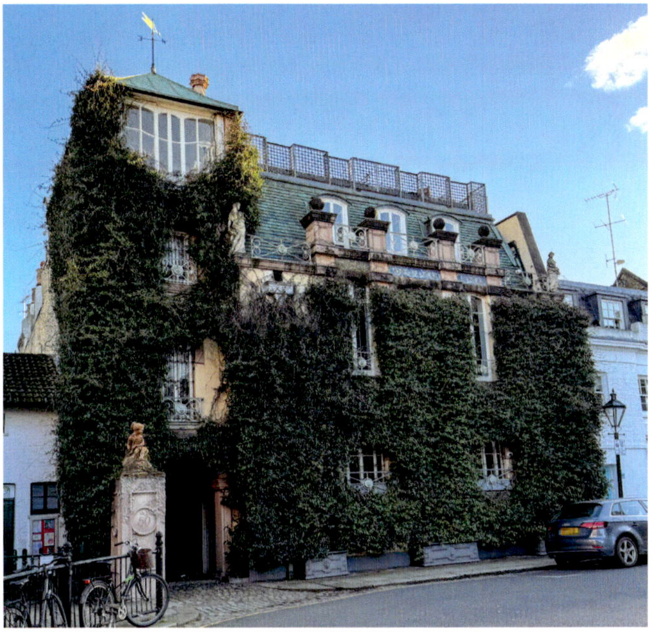

Right: No. 50 Glebe Place.

Below: Glebe Studios.

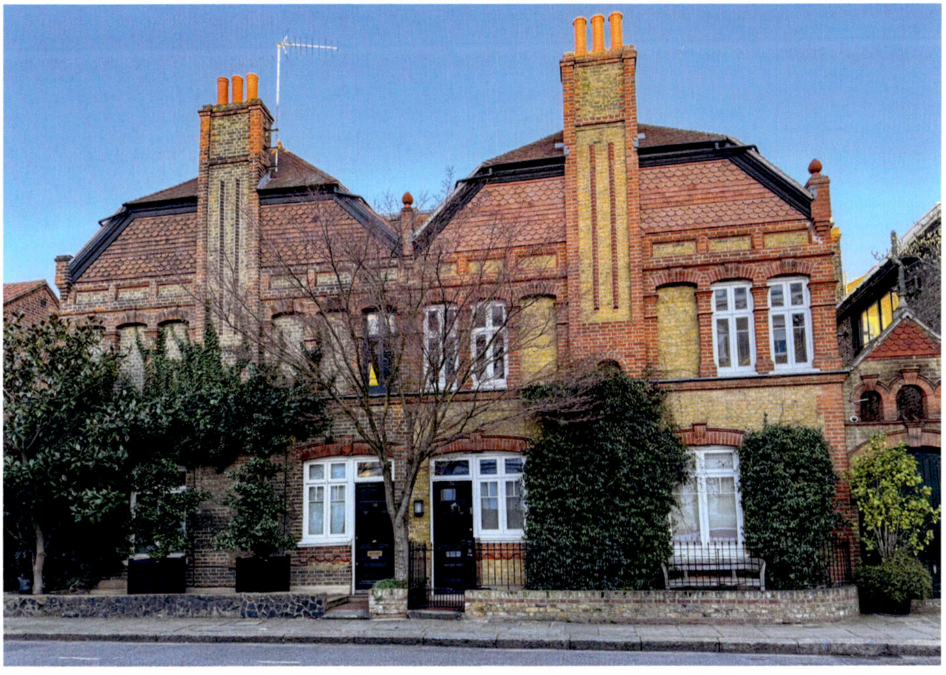

Despite its 'old' appearance and ivy façade adorned with statues, plaques and a date of '1723' on its gutter hopper, No. 50 Glebe Place was only constructed in the late 1980s. An imposing house with a roof garden it was built for the advertising baron, Sir Frank Lowe.

19. The Cadogan Arms, No. 298 King's Road, SW3

The initial pub on this site was called the Rose and Crown and built in the seventeenth century. However, today's structure dates to the 1830s when the earlier pub was rebuilt and renamed the Cadogan Arms, in recognition of the Cadogan family's association with the parish of Chelsea. The pub sits on the corner of Old Church Street and the King's Road and has an exterior full of colourful floral displays. Recently renovated the inside has been returned to its former glory and boasts beautiful wooden panelling, a hand-carved bar, glazed tiles, fireplaces and comfy deep armchairs. It is nowadays one of Chelsea's most popular pubs, which not only offers an excellent range of beers, fine wines and cocktails but also simple British cuisine including oysters and mussels as well as fish and chips in its luxuriously decorated restaurant below the main bar.

The Cadogan Estate owes it origins to Sir Hans Sloane, who as Chelsea's lord of the manor owned much of the manor's land. Following his death in 1753 his estate passed to his daughters, one of whom was married to Baron Cadogan of Oakley. Their union resulted in the management of Chelsea passing to the Cadogan family, which ultimately became responsible for a greater part of the manor – about 270 acres in size. It was George, the 5th Earl Cadogan, who perhaps made the greatest impact on the area when he led a major redevelopment

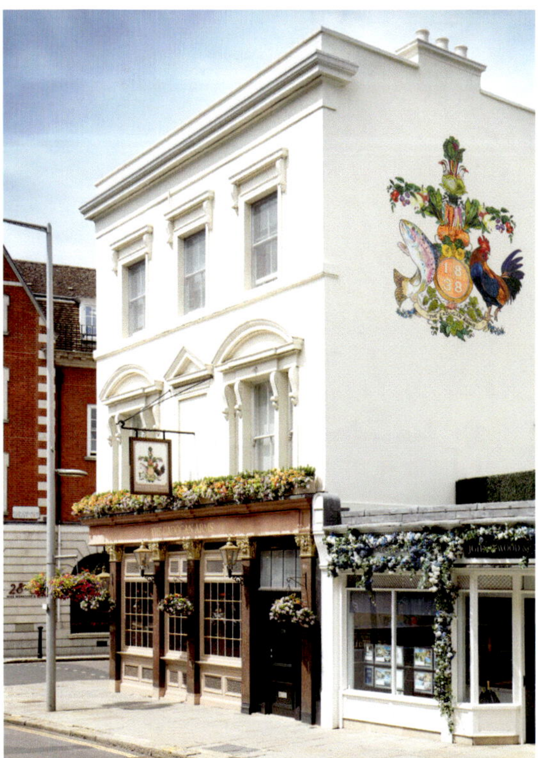

Left and opposite: The Cadogan Arms.

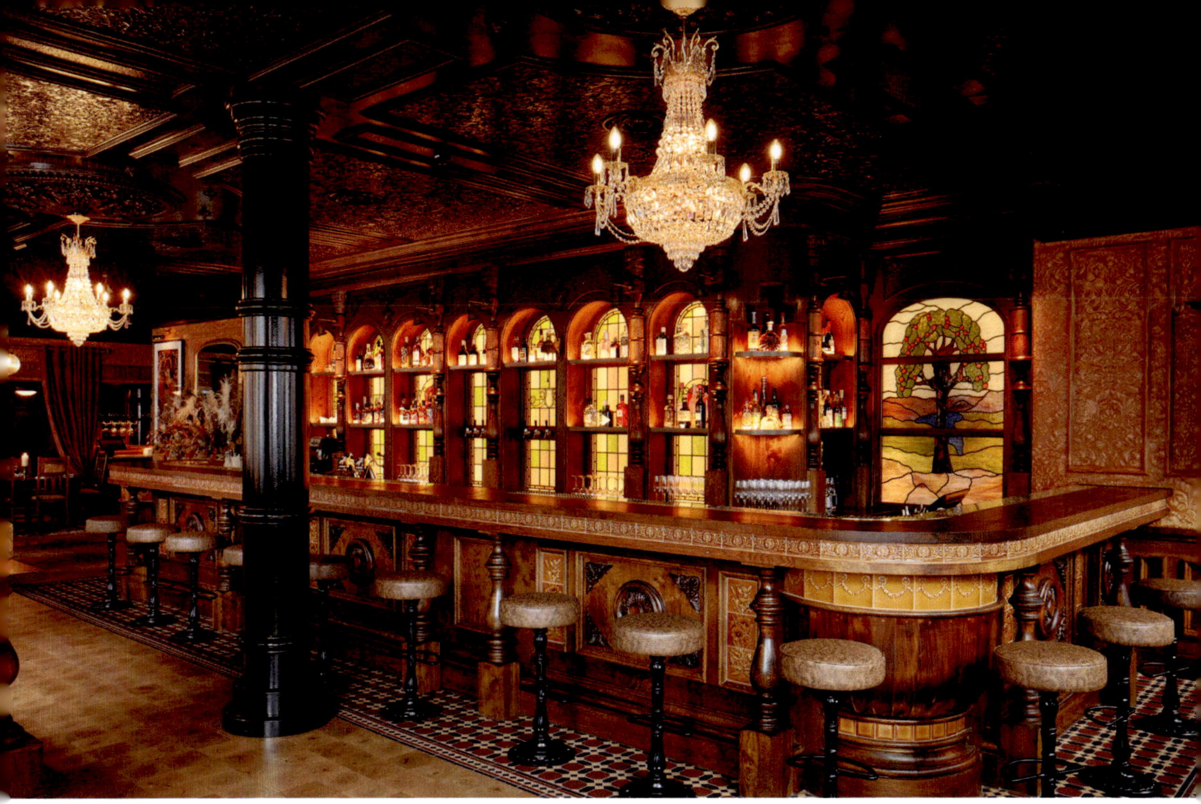

of the estate in the late nineteenth century, resulting in the construction of Hans Town with its new, revolutionary style of architecture. He was heavily involved in Chelsea, as its first elected mayor, and in politics too where he served under Disraeli and Salisbury in the governments of the day. Today the Cadogan Estate continues to play a major part in shaping Chelsea's future and has a portfolio that includes residential, leisure and commercial properties as well as green spaces. It frequently donates money to local and national charities and is totally committed to conserving the heritage of Chelsea and ensuring a sustainable environment.

https://thecadoganarms.london

20. The Royal Court Theatre, Sloane Square, SW3

A major feature of Sloane Square and one of London's most loved theatres, the Royal Court has occupied this site since 1888. Located beside Sloane Square Tube station it is an imposing ornate red-brick and stone building designed in the Italian Renaissance style which fits in well with the Flemish and Dutch style of architecture in many of Chelsea's surrounding streets. Despite still bearing its original façade, the theatre's interior has been altered several times during its lifetime, most recently in the late 1990s when it attracted funding from the Arts Council and from the newly formed Lottery Fund. It was a long overdue renovation which vastly improved the fabric of the building and yet retained its Victorian character. Today's Royal

Court offers two performance spaces: the Jerwood Theatre Upstairs, a small and intimate space, and the larger 400-seat Jerwood Theatre Downstairs. There is also an atmospheric café and small shop in the basement area.

Initially the Royal Court was known for light entertainment, but this all changed when Harley Granville-Barker and J. E. Vedrenne arrived at the theatre in the early 1900s. They extended the theatre's repertoire to include works of a more controversial nature and sought out plays that were both stimulating and challenging. In fact, under their watch the theatre put on plays by John Galsworthy as well as eleven of George Bernard Shaw's works. However, competition from the cinema resulted in the theatre's closure in 1932. It reopened in the 1950s under the management of the English Stage Company with George Devine as artistic director. Under his direction ambitious British and foreign plays were staged, especially those with thought-provoking themes, as John Osborne's *Look Back in Anger*. His later play *A Patriot for Me* was deemed inappropriate by the Lord Chamberlain's office (responsible for censorship at the time) and was refused a performance licence. This caused such furore that to circumvent the ruling the theatre turned itself into a private members' club for the duration of the run.

The Royal Court today thrives and continues on its mission to promote new, unknown and emerging playwrights from Britain and overseas.

www.royalcourttheatre.com

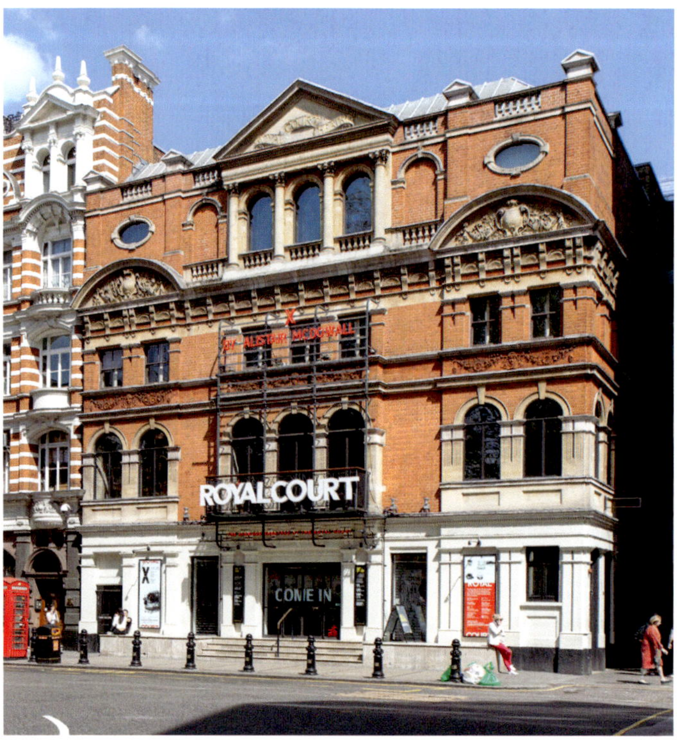

The Royal Court Theatre.

21. River Crossings: Battersea, Chelsea and Albert Bridges, SW3

The first of Chelsea's crossings was Battersea Bridge, a wooden bridge built in the early 1770s. Two more crossings connecting Chelsea with Battersea were built in 1858 (Chelsea) and 1872 (Albert).

When Chelsea Bridge was being built workmen excavating the riverbed made an amazing discovery when they unearthed what is perhaps the most significant piece of art from the Celtic period, the Battersea Shield. The shield consists of a magnificent bronze facing adorned with twenty-seven red glass 'enamel'-framed studs and is now displayed in the British Museum. It is thought to be a ceremonial shield from the Iron Age, most probably used as an offering. Historians believe that the site where it was found is probably where Julius Caesar crossed the river in 54 BC and may account for the human bones and weapons uncovered hereabouts.

The first Battersea bridge was considered to be a romantic structure and was captured in the works of many nineteenth-century artists such as Whistler, Turner and Greaves. However, maintenance costs resulted in a new bridge being built in 1890. This bridge remains in use today but has been criticised for being uninteresting and less picturesque than the earlier bridge.

Chelsea Bridge that sits beside Battersea Power Station is also a replacement of the original suspension bridge and was constructed in 1937. Originally called the Victoria Bridge after Queen Victoria, it was renamed as the authorities, concerned about the

Battersea Bridge.

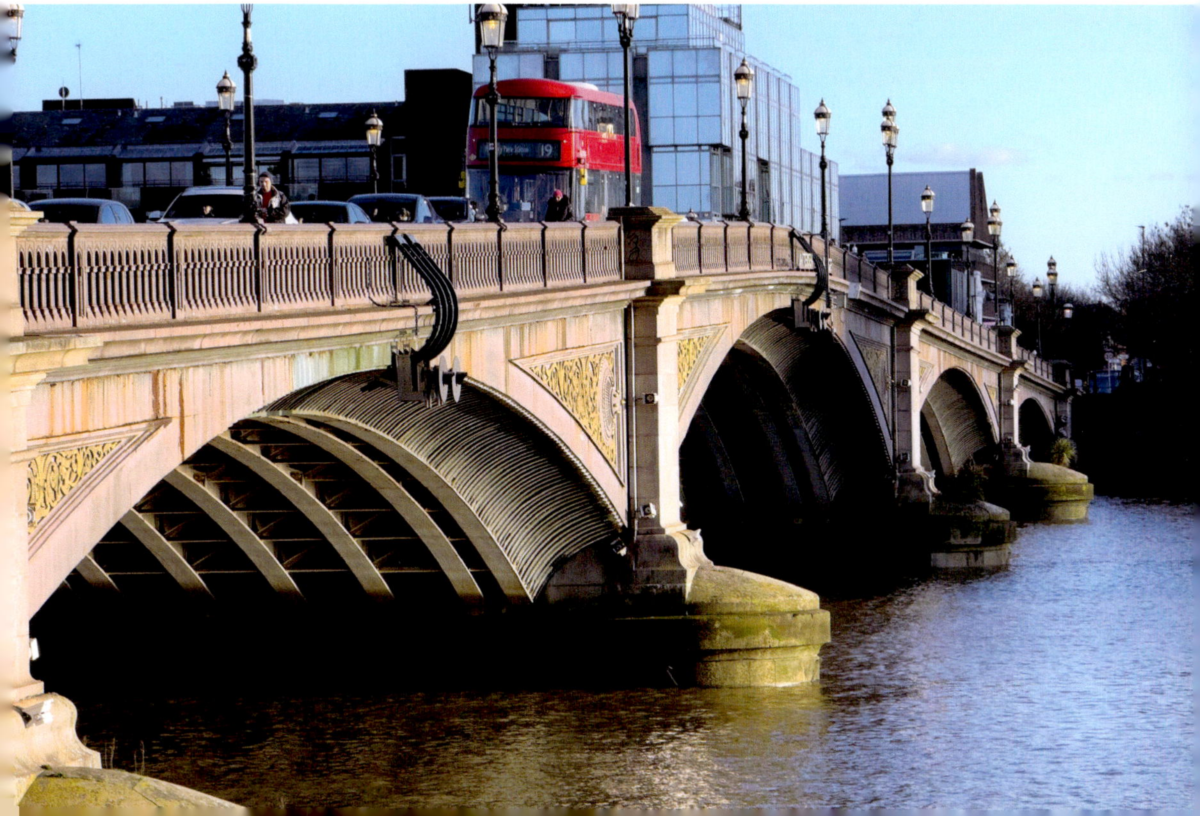

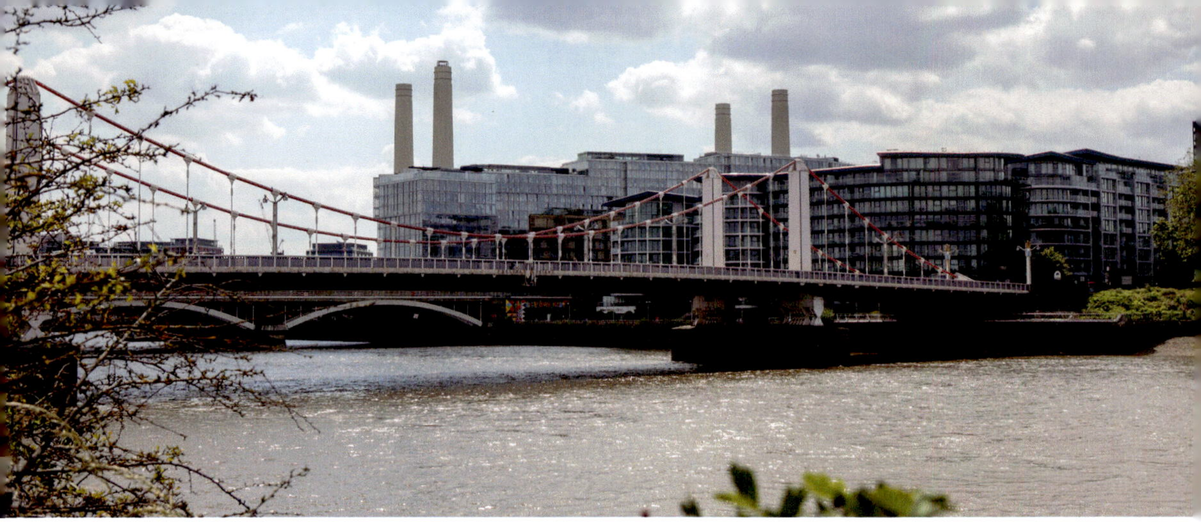

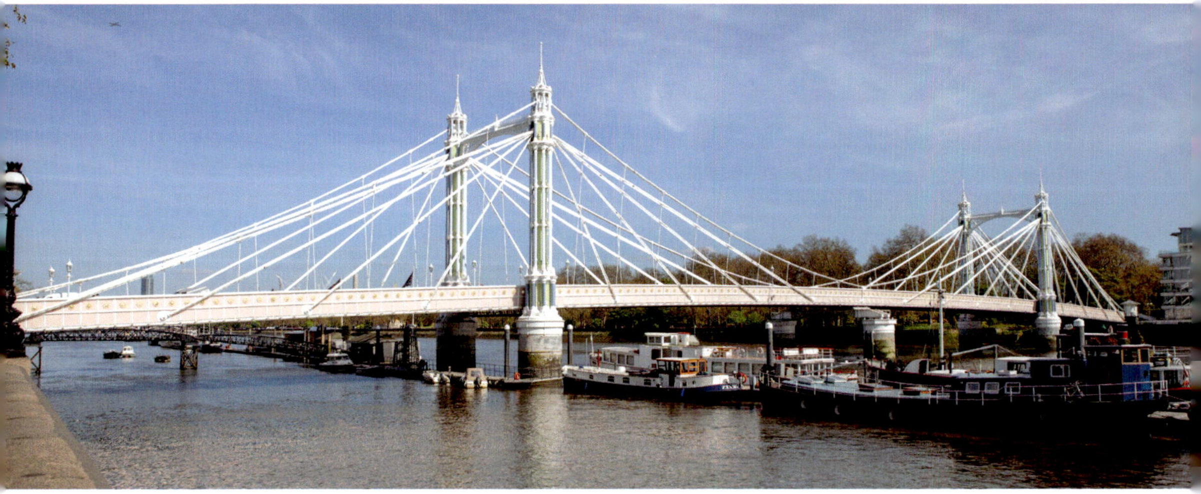

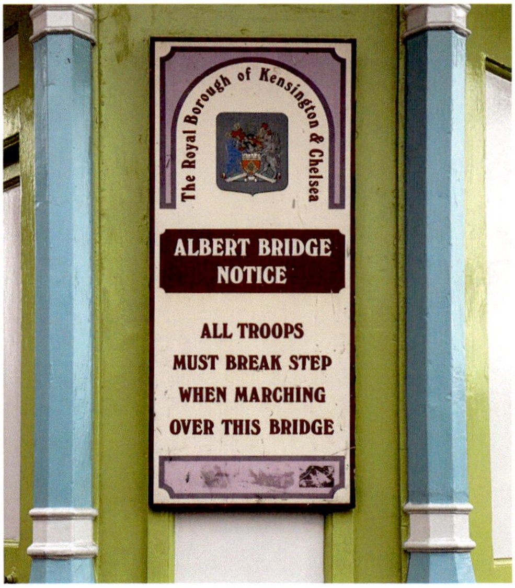

Top: Chelsea Bridge.

Above: Albert Bridge.

Left: Sign on Albert Bridge.

bridge's safety did not want the queen's name to be associated with its possible future collapse. This new bridge, like its predecessor, was a suspension bridge, but was unique in being the first self-anchored suspension bridge in the country.

The third crossing, Albert Bridge is one of London's prettiest bridges and easily spotted for its elegant painted exterior in pink, blue and green. It is the only bridge in the city to have retained its original tollbooths and is beautifully lit at night. Due to the vibrations felt when large numbers of pedestrians crossed at the same time, it was nicknamed the 'Trembling Lady' when first built. Look out for the notices reminding troops 'to break step when crossing the bridge'.

22. Norman Shaw Buildings, Nos 9–17 Chelsea Embankment, SW3

The Chelsea Embankment is renowned for its string of imposing, lofty and individualistic houses designed by the Victorian and Edwardian architect (Richard) Norman Shaw (1831–1912).

Facing Battersea Park, these stunning red-brick houses were built in the late 1870s and are noted for their contrasting white stonework as well as their variety, shape and size of windows, gables, iron balconies, railings, high chimneys and overhanging floors.

Shaw was responsible for Nos 8–11, 15, 17–18 Chelsea Embankment and each house has its own distinct character. No. 17 (Swan House) is perhaps the most well-known and is easy to identify due to the graceful pair of swans that adorn its main entrance door. Now a Grade II* listed building, it was built by Shaw between 1875 and 1876 as a home for Wickham Flower, an art collector, and his artist wife. Shaw's use of dormer, narrow and caged oriel and bay windows on the building's frontage is simply unique. In the early 1980s Swan House was the headquarters of Securicor and it was here in 1981 that wedding gifts for Prince Charles and Lady Diana Spencer were kept in storage. It later became an architectural studio, but in the early 2000s was converted into a luxurious private home with its own basement swimming pool, terraces, ballroom and cinema.

The Clock House at No. 8 Chelsea Embankment also features interesting and wide oriel windows. Nikolaus Pevsner, the architectural historian, notes that Clock House's broad façade is entirely symmetrical apart from the clock, which hangs to the right of the main entrance on the first floor.

No. 18, known as Cheyne House, on the corner of Chelsea Embankment and Royal Hospital Road, has a superb, curved ground floor and in keeping with Shaw's other houses has striking features and windows in abundance. It too has been converted into residential use in recent times.

Shaw's work was influenced by the Gothic Revival architect G. E. Street as well as Philip Webb, who pioneered the Queen Anne Revival style in the early 1870s. Although not an innovator himself, Shaw interpreted this style, using it to create his own personal and distinctive urban design.

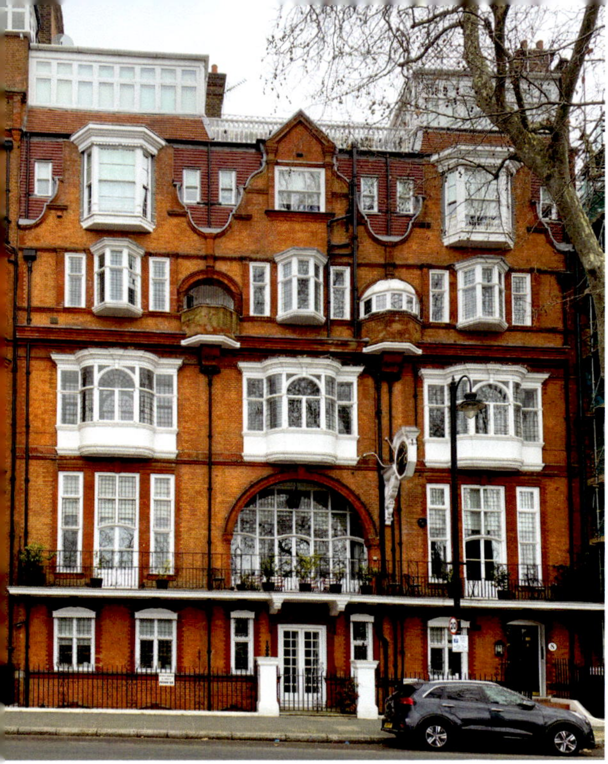

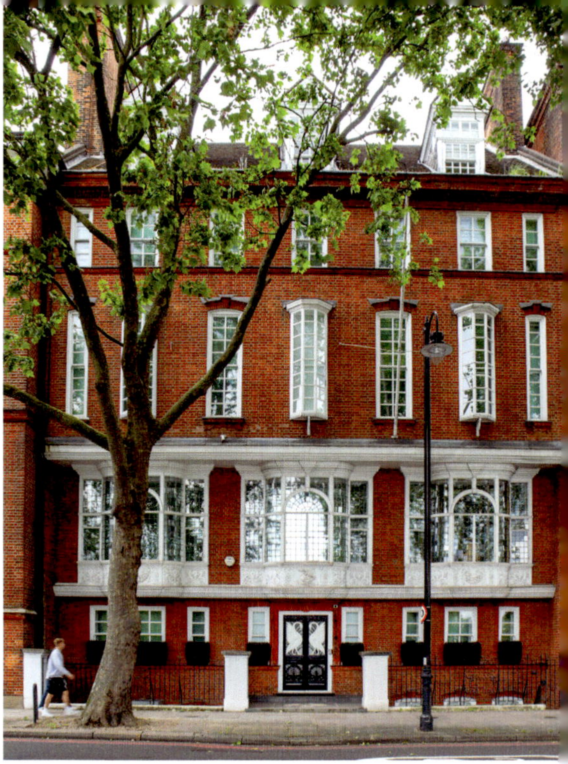

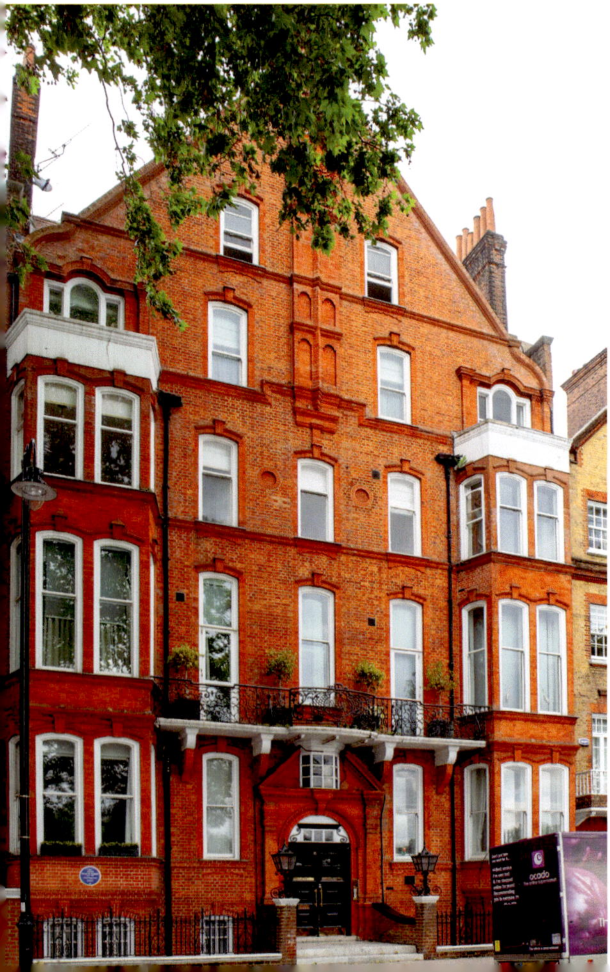

Above left: Clock House.

Above right: Swan House.

Left: No. 15 Chelsea Embankment.

23. Tite Street Houses: Artistic and Literary Hub, SW3

This seemingly quiet and respectable residential street was once the epicentre of Chelsea's artistic, literary and aesthetic scene, known not only for its multitude of artists' studios but also for the scandalous behaviour of some of its colourful residents. It was certainly both radical and bohemian, and attracted not only artists, their mistresses and muses but also wealthy patrons who came to sit for their portraits here. The late nineteenth century witnessed a great change in Chelsea: the Chelsea Embankment was developed with sizeable properties for the rich, and there was a huge boom in housing construction nearby. Tite Street, providing access from the Chelsea Embankment towards the King's Road, was an ideal location for artists and writers to settle; its proximity to the river was a valuable asset (many artists drew inspiration from the Thames) and the street was filled with affordable sites.

The first artist to build a house here was the American-born James McNeill Whistler. Known as the 'White House' it was designed by E. W. Godwin with a studio on the top floor and a 'school' below. Sadly, Whistler lived here for only a short period as his libel case against the art critic Ruskin bankrupted him and he was forced to sell up. John Singer Sargent, also an American expat, took up residence at No. 33 Tite Street where he lived for twenty-four years.

John Singer Sargent's house.

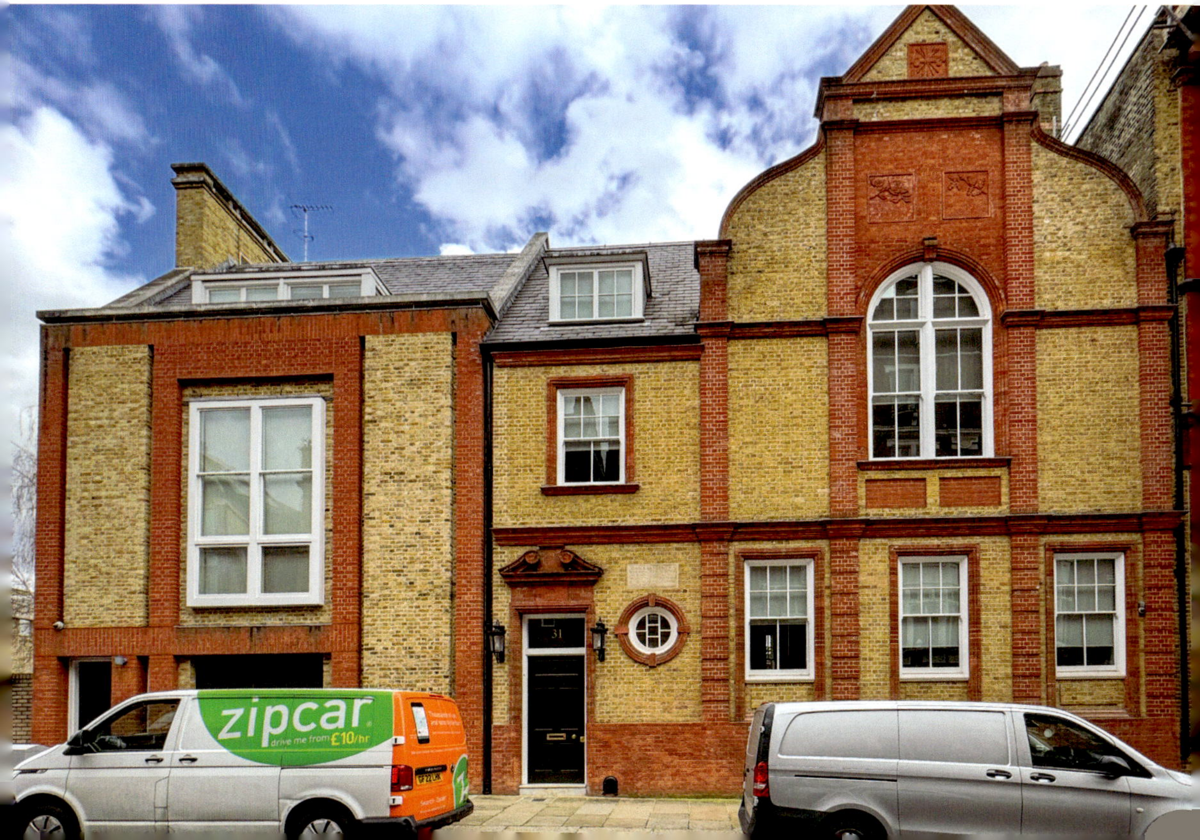

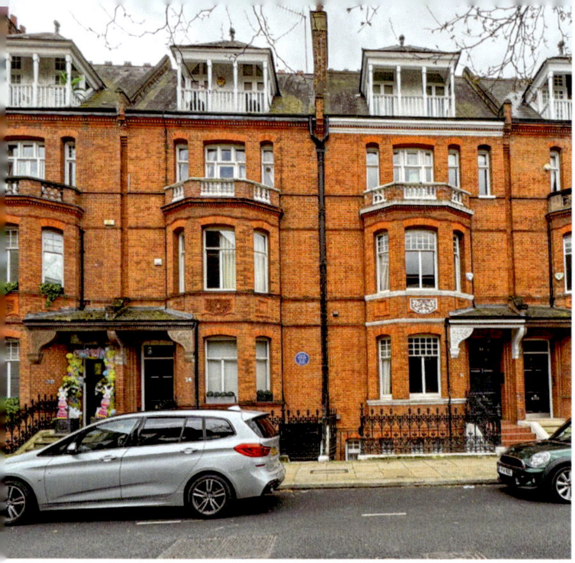

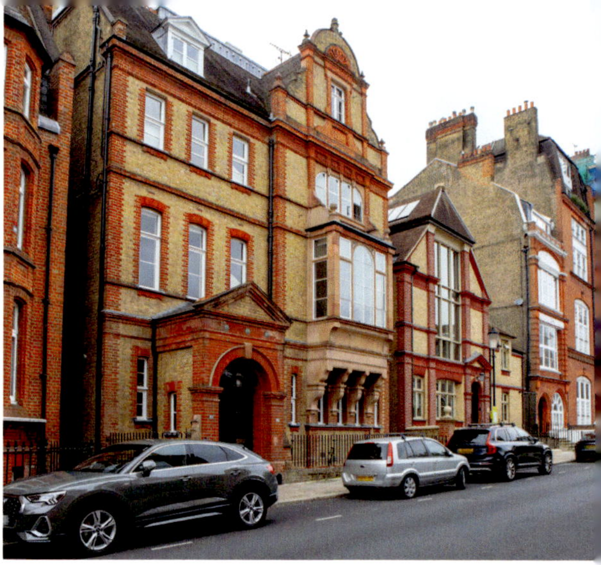

Above left: Oscar Wilde's house.

Above right: Artists' studio houses, Tite Street.

An incredibly prolific and popular portrait painter, his studio was constantly filled with famous names, including the actress Ellen Terry. One morning in 1889 she arrived at his house to attend a sitting dressed as Lady Macbeth with flowing long red hair and emerald robes. Oscar Wilde, who lived opposite, saw the scene and was captivated by the sight. Wilde had bought No. 34 when he married in 1884, and it was here that he wrote many of his famous plays and the novel *The Picture of Dorian Gray* (1891). He lived here with his family until his trial for gross indecency in 1895.

In the 1990s Diana, Princess of Wales and Margaret Thatcher both sat at No. 33 for portraits by the artist Nelson Shanks.

24. Carlyle Mansions, Cheyne Walk, SW3

Carlyle Mansions is a monumental block of flats named after the Scottish philosopher and essayist Thomas Carlyle, who had lived nearby in the nineteenth century (see Building 8). It is a particularly striking red-brick building that occupies a large corner plot between Cheyne Row and Lawrence Street. Built in 1886 it is six storeys high and is charmingly embellished on its western side by Portland stone relief panels that feature birds and flowers that stand out well against the brickwork. The mansion block very quickly acquired the nickname 'The Writers' Block' due to the great number of eminent and distinguished writers who have lived there.

Flat 21 was home to Henry James from 1913 until his death in 1916. Some years later the writer T. S. Eliot moved into the block, and it was here that his plays *The Cocktail Party* (1949) and *The Confidential Clerk* (1953) were penned. Ian Fleming, another famous writer, took up residence in 1950 and wrote the

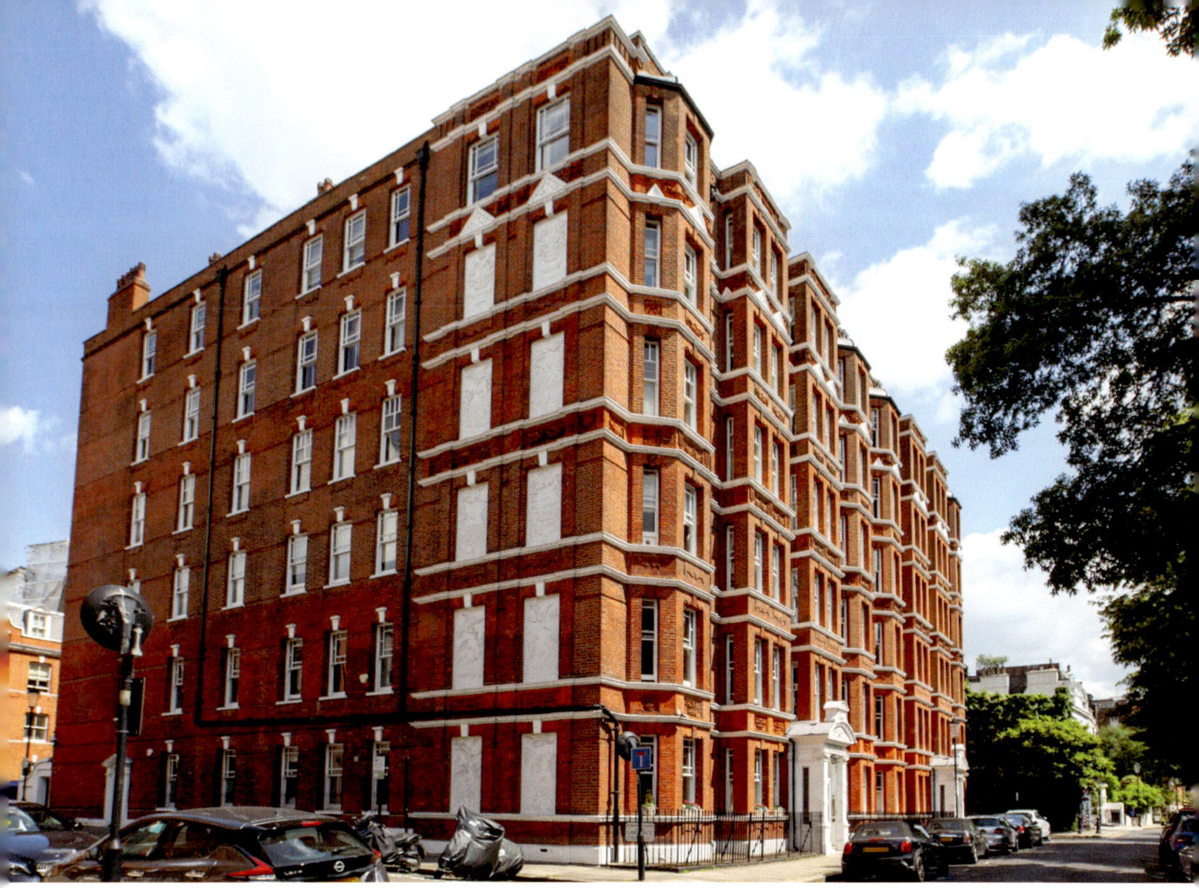

Above: Carlyle Mansions.

Below: Stone relief panels on Carlyle Mansions.

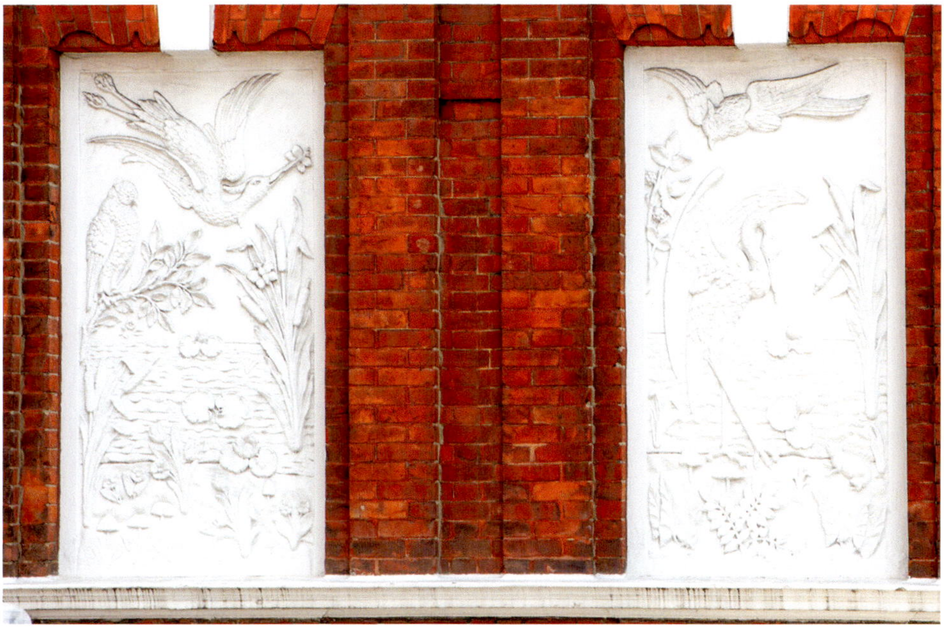

draft of his novel *Casino Royale,* the first in his 007 series about James Bond, the suave British spy.

Other well-known writers to have lived here include W. Somerset Maugham and Robert Erskine Childers.

25. Cadogan Hotel, No. 75 Sloane Street, SW3

The Cadogan opened on Sloane Street in 1887 as a fabulously sumptuous hotel located midway between Sloane Square and Knightsbridge. The hotel's architecture in the new Queen Anne style was built in red brick and white stone, embellished with carved stonework, high chimneys and turrets, and it immediately became a fashionable venue for artists, writers and intellectuals. Since opening, the hotel has played host to numerous celebrities and has been the scene of one of the country's most notorious arrests of the late nineteenth century. In the 1980s the hotel attracted many stars including the supermodels of the day. In fact, it has often been associated with the rich and decadent and has had quite a dramatic history. Nowadays, it falls under the umbrella of the Belmond group of luxury hotels and continues its reputation for opulence and stylishness in both a classic and contemporary way. The Cadogan has grown over its lifetime and now extends over five properties – three in Sloane Street and two in Pont Street. The latter greatly complement the former and are constructed in warm terracotta with magnificent gables, chimneys,

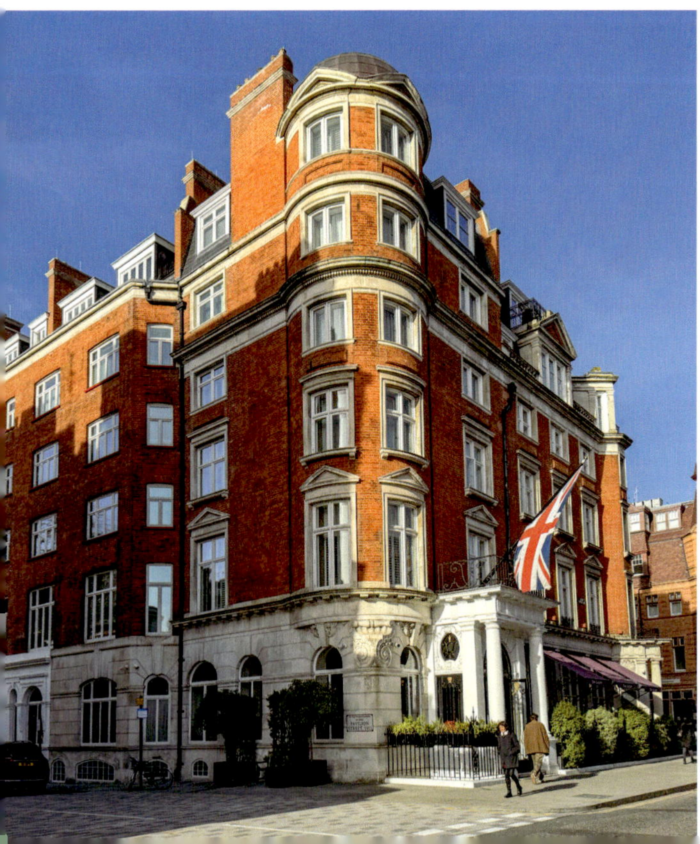

Left and opposite: Cadogan Hotel.

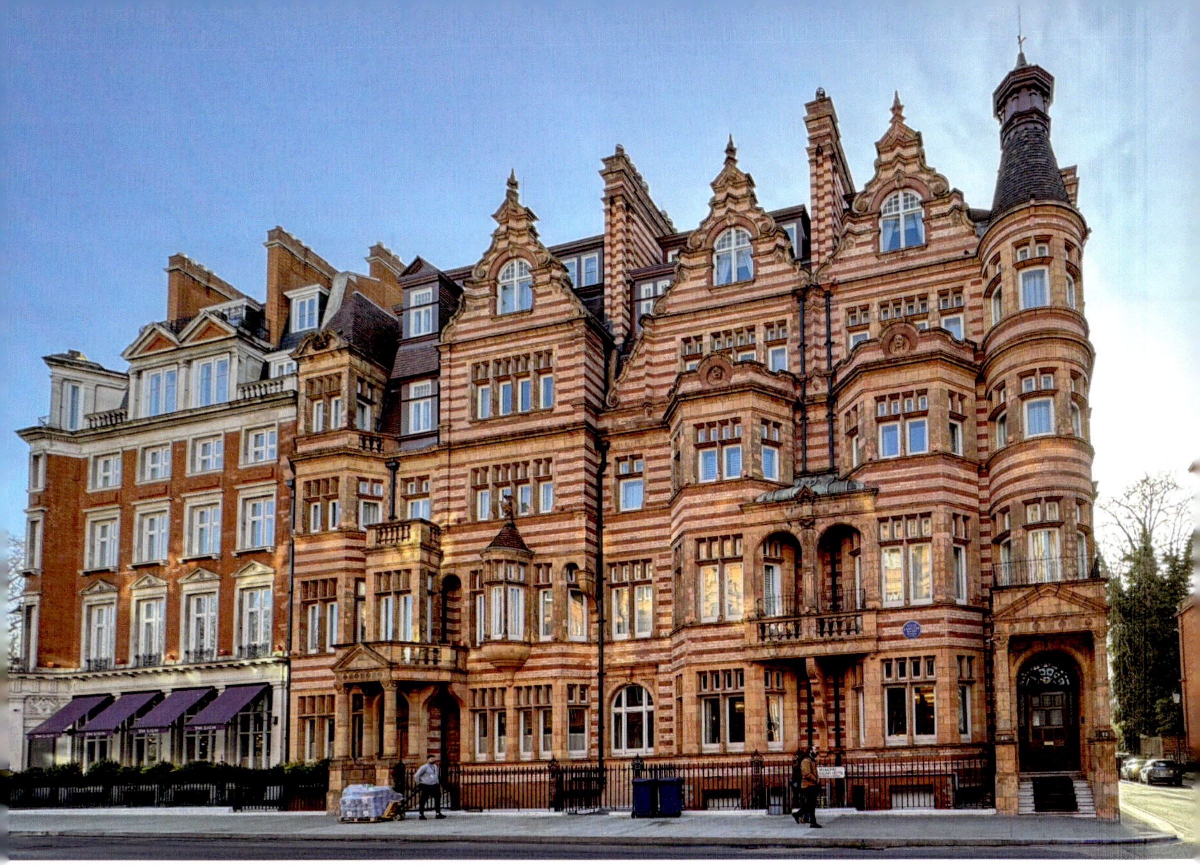

balconies and corner towers and are an excellent example of the Pont Street Dutch style of architecture. One of these, No. 21, was where in the 1890s Lillie Langtry, the actress and mistress of the Prince of Wales (later Edward VII), lived and socialised and it is said where she entertained the Prince of Wales in secret. When her house was absorbed by the Cadogan in 1895 the hotel agreed that she could remain living there for free in what had been her old rooms – today's room 106.

Another frequent customer of the hotel at this time was the flamboyant wit and writer Oscar Wilde. He used the hotel as his pied-à-terre and often stayed overnight in room 118. Here, Wilde would spend hours with Chelsea's elite talking, smoking cigars and drinking long into the night. It was in this room that Wilde was arrested for gross indecency on 6 April 1895 and later served two years' hard labour in Reading Gaol for his crime.

www.belmond.com/hotels/europe/uk/london/belmond-cadogan-hotel

26. Hans Town and Cadogan Square, SW1

When Henry Holland acquired building rights on around 100 acres of Lord Cadogan's land in 1771, he christened the district Hans Town. This was in honour of Cadogan's father-in-law, Sir Hans Sloane, who had been lord of the manor and was one of Chelsea's greatest benefactors. Holland's intention was to create a fashionable residential estate centred around Pont Street and Hans Place with modest-sized housing that would appeal mainly to tradespeople such as milliners, hairdressers and dressmakers. The houses, built largely in terraces, were two to three storeys high with attics and basements and of typical Georgian design with fanlights and sash windows. When the leases began to run out in the late nineteenth century, trends in architecture were changing and this led to the complete redevelopment of Hans Town into the 'Red Rose City' that we have today.

In the late 1870s and 1880s a large square, Cadogan Square, was built where Holland's own magnificent villa had once stood. This quickly became a showpiece of everything associated with the new Queen Anne Revival style of architecture, which introduced red brick to Hans Town. The revolutionary style with its extremely tall, ornately carved brickwork, balconies, steeply pitched roofs and shaped gables was utterly different. Many houses had features more commonly

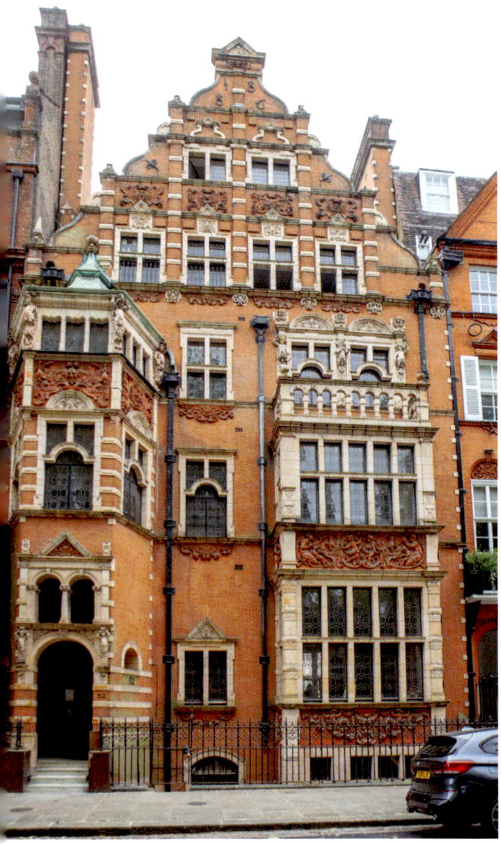

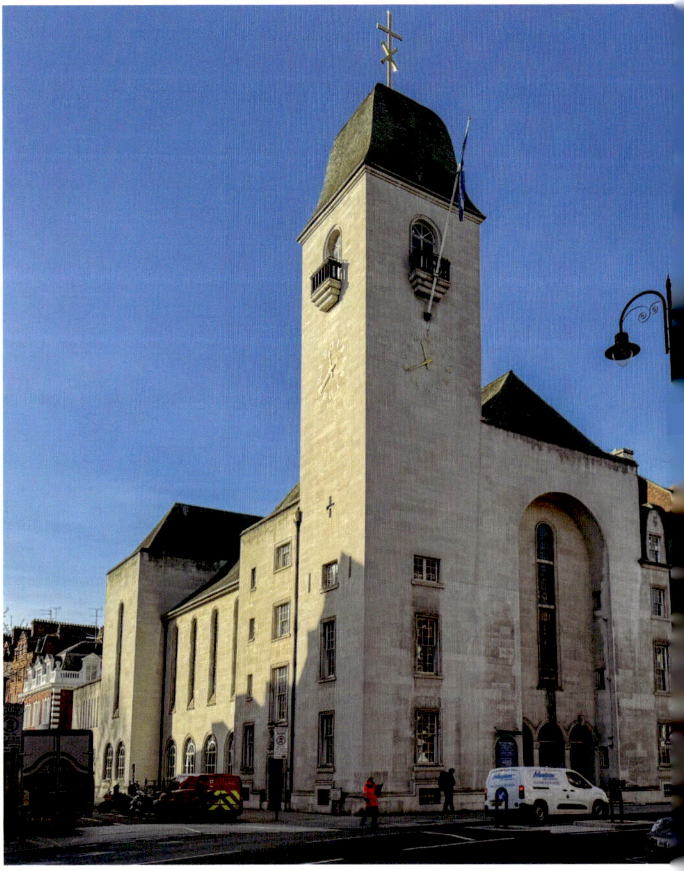

Above left: No. 52 Cadogan Square.

Above right: St Columba's Church.

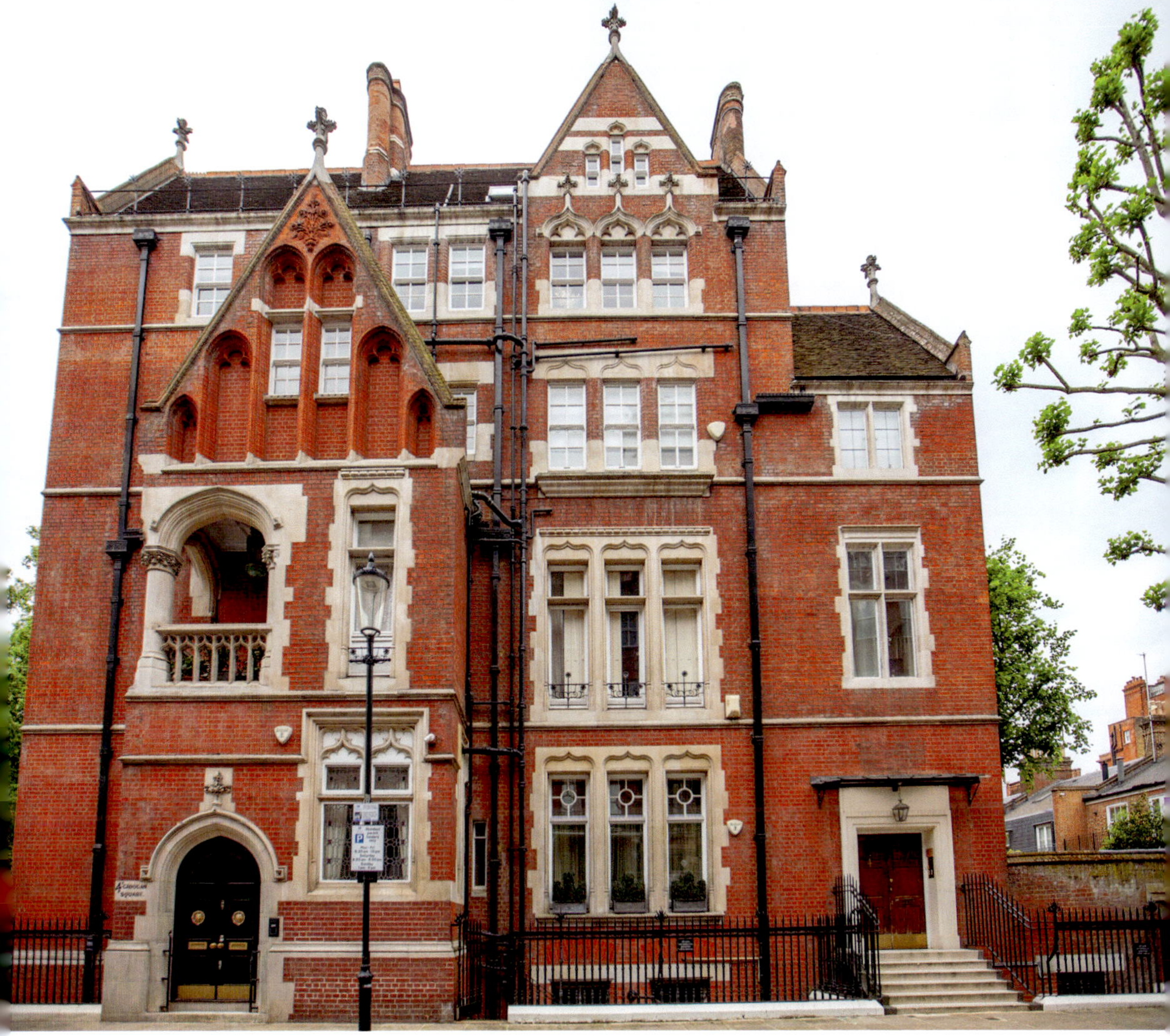

No. 4 Cadogan Square.

seen on the canal-side houses in Amsterdam, Bruges and Antwerp and because of these influences the enclave became known as 'Pont Street Dutch'.

The new housing was aimed at the affluent classes, so it is hardly surprising that the greatest architects of the day were involved in their design. On the western side of Cadogan Square there are excellent examples of R. Norman Shaw's unique style at Nos 62, 68 and 72 while Ernest George and G. A. Peto's eye-catching building at No. 52 using terracotta mouldings and ornate leaded lights is simply outstanding. George Street's own home at No. 4 Cadogan Square is particularly unusual for its Gothic design.

Although Cadogan Square may appear uniform, it has the footprints of many celebrated Victorian architects, and on closer observation one sees great variations in design. Furthermore, not all of Hans Town is built in red brick, as is demonstrated by Pont Street's iconic St Columba's Church that is built in Portland stone with a green slate roof.

27. Chelsea Old Town Hall, Nos 165–179 King's Road, SW3

One of Chelsea's most recognised buildings, Chelsea Old Town Hall sits on the corner of Chelsea Manor Street and the King's Road. Its stunning entrance on the King's Road, with its sweep of marble stairs leading to a porch embellished with columns and a pediment above, is often the place where brides and grooms gather to have their photos taken. Many glamorous and famous people have exchanged wedding vows here, including celebrity chef Marco Pierre White; actors Judy Garland, Pierce Brosnan, Roman Polanski and Sharon Tate; as well as the footballer Patrick Vieira. In 2014 a mass of journalists gathered around the town hall believing that the actor and film director George Clooney and his fiancée, local barrister Amal Alamuddin, were about to be married here. It was all to no avail as the pair were miles away in Venice where their ceremony took place at a luxury resort. A marriage of significance that occurred within the town hall in 1928 was that of the American Wallis Spencer to her second husband, Ernest Simpson. It was because of Wallis Simpson's earlier marriages and divorces that Edward VIII took the decision to abdicate from the throne in 1936.

Chelsea Old Town Hall is so named as it ceased to function as Chelsea's administrative centre when the Royal Borough of Kensington and Chelsea was created in 1965. The present building, housing the Sports Centre, Chelsea Library, the Register Office and some splendidly decorated Edwardian halls and suites, was built between 1906 and 1908. It was designed by the architect Leonard Stokes and is a most impressive municipal building in the early English baroque style. Largely

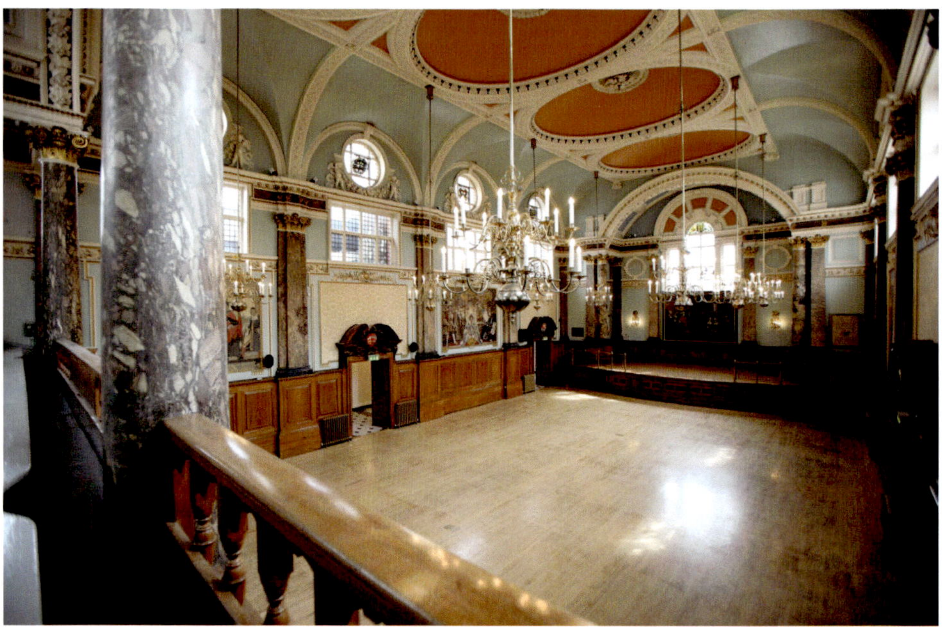

Chelsea Old Town Hall. (© Royal Borough of Kensington & Chelsea)

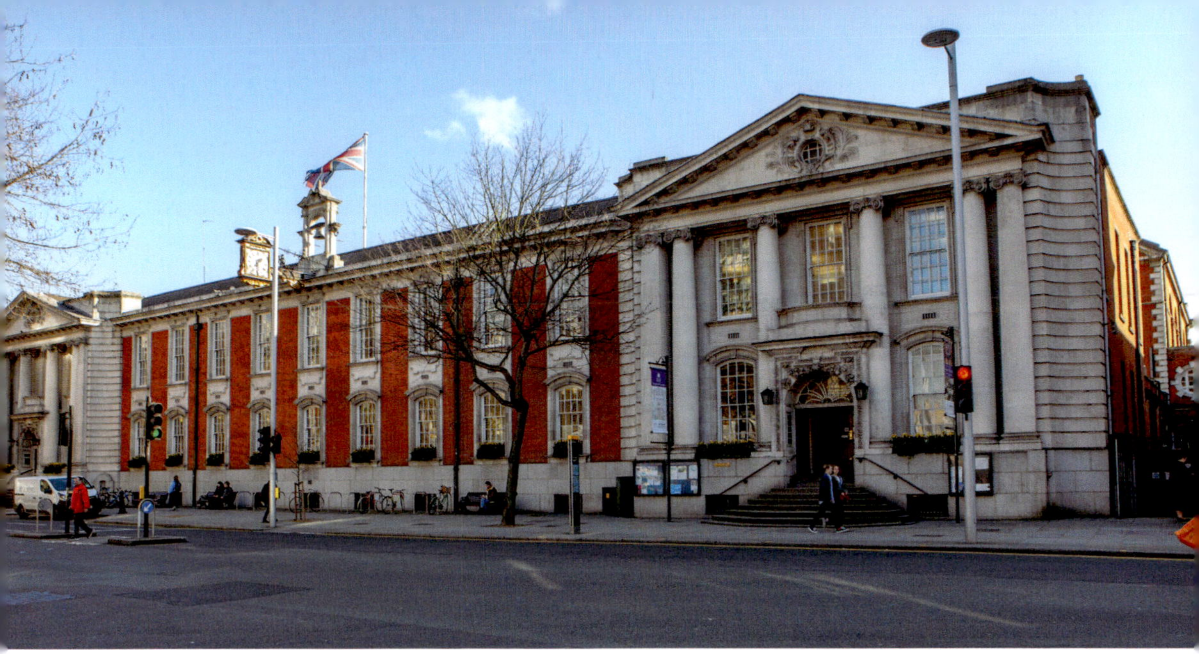

Chelsea Old Town Hall.

built in red brick, it has symmetrical stone entrances at either end with pediments above and, at the building's centre, a bellcote, in front of which hangs an imposing black and gold clock. This building, however, was not the first Chelsea Town Hall, having incorporated an earlier building of 1886–87, designed by John Brydon, with an entrance on Chelsea Manor Street. This earlier town hall had taken the place of the original King's Road Chelsea Vestry Hall of 1858 (which at that time contained a scientific institution as well as public baths).

www.rbkc.gov.uk

28. Holy Trinity Church, Sloane Street, SW3

Dubbed by the Poet Laureate Sir John Betjeman the 'Cathedral of the Arts and Crafts Movement', Holy Trinity Church is to all intents and purposes an utter work of art. It contains many marvellous treasures of the artists, sculptors and glassmakers associated with the movement and today has Grade I listed status. Designed in the late 1880s by the art architect John Dando Sedding with a polychromatic stripy red-brick and stone exterior, Holy Trinity Church took the place of a much smaller church that had been erected some sixty years earlier. The new church, funded by the 5th Earl Cadogan, was necessary to provide the ever-increasing populace with a large enough place to worship and at the same time was fitting in its size and ornamentation for the high-class residents of the newly established Hans Town.

Sedding, a prime force in the Arts and Crafts movement, was greatly influenced by Pugin and Ruskin and was trained by one of the Victorian era's most admired and leading ecclesiastical architects, G. E. Street. His work in Holy Trinity displays

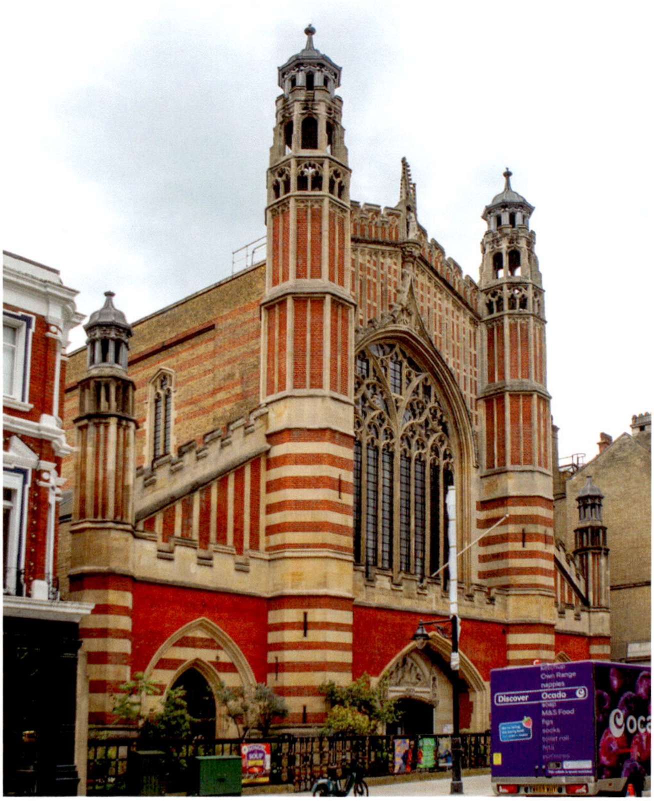

Left and below right: Holy Trinity Church.

Below left: Holy Trinity Church. (© Effiong Onoyom)

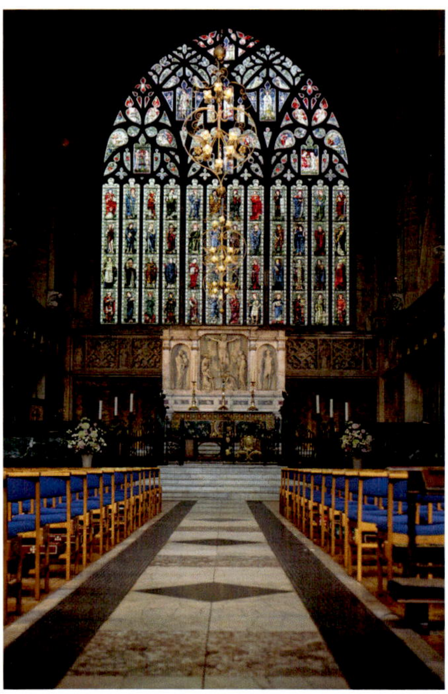

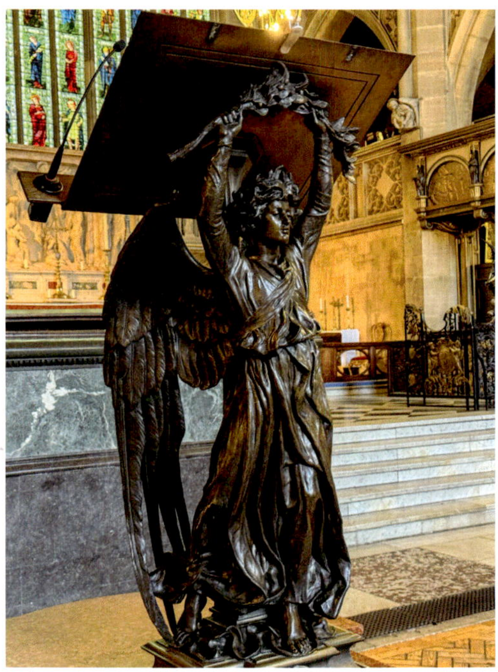

the influence of the Arts and Crafts movement and its desire to preserve hand craftsmanship and to use traditional designs and building techniques. The church Sedding designed is simply awe-inspiring not only for its height, size and width but for the beauty of its marble, stained-glass collection, ironwork, chandeliers and sculptures. The skill of the sculptors Pomeroy, Onslow Ford, John Tweed, Hamo Thornycroft and H. H. Armstead are displayed throughout Holy Trinity, as are the excellent stained-glass windows crafted by William Blake Richmond and Christopher Whall in the north and south aisles. The pièce de résistance must however be the stunning east window with its forty-eight panels depicting saints, the work of Edward Burne-Jones and William Morris. It was Morris & Co.'s largest ever window to be manufactured, which may well have prevented the church's demolition in the 1970s following wartime damage.

When Sedding died in 1891 much of Holy Trinity's ornamentation was added by his successor, Henry Wilson, and although not all the planned additions were carried out, the ultimate effect was and still is quite magnificent.

www.sloanechurch.org

29. Peter Jones Department Store, Sloane Square, SW3

The store takes its name from its Welsh founder Peter Rees Jones, who built up his business as a draper in London, moving into the King's Road in 1877. As he became increasingly successful, he bought up all the neighbouring premises which resulted in a long row of shops. His next step was to erect just one building on the site. Considered avant-garde for the time, his new store built in red-brick and stone with a green slate roof had electric lighting, luxurious wooden show cabinets and operated a fleet of horse-drawn vans to deliver merchandise to nearby residents. The store was bought by another draper, John Lewis of Oxford Street, on Jones's death in 1905. The new proprietor was so keen to procure it that it is said he walked from the West End with £20,000 in cash to guarantee the purchase!

Lewis's eldest son, John Spedan Lewis, took over the store's management in 1906 and eight years later, total control. It was he who introduced the idea of a profit-sharing partnership (much to his father's disapproval) which was finally adopted across all the John Lewis stores in 1929. It was in the mid-1920s that the slogan 'Never Knowingly Undersold' became a price pledge of John Lewis and it is only very recently that the partnership has discontinued it due to the change in national retail buying trends.

Peter Jones underwent total redevelopment in the 1930s which caused a good deal of controversy when the new building was unveiled. Designed by William Crabtree it was built in the popular modernist style, and many likened it to an ocean liner with its striking curtain wall made of glass and steel. The new store benefited from brighter and greater internal space and the curve of the wall was

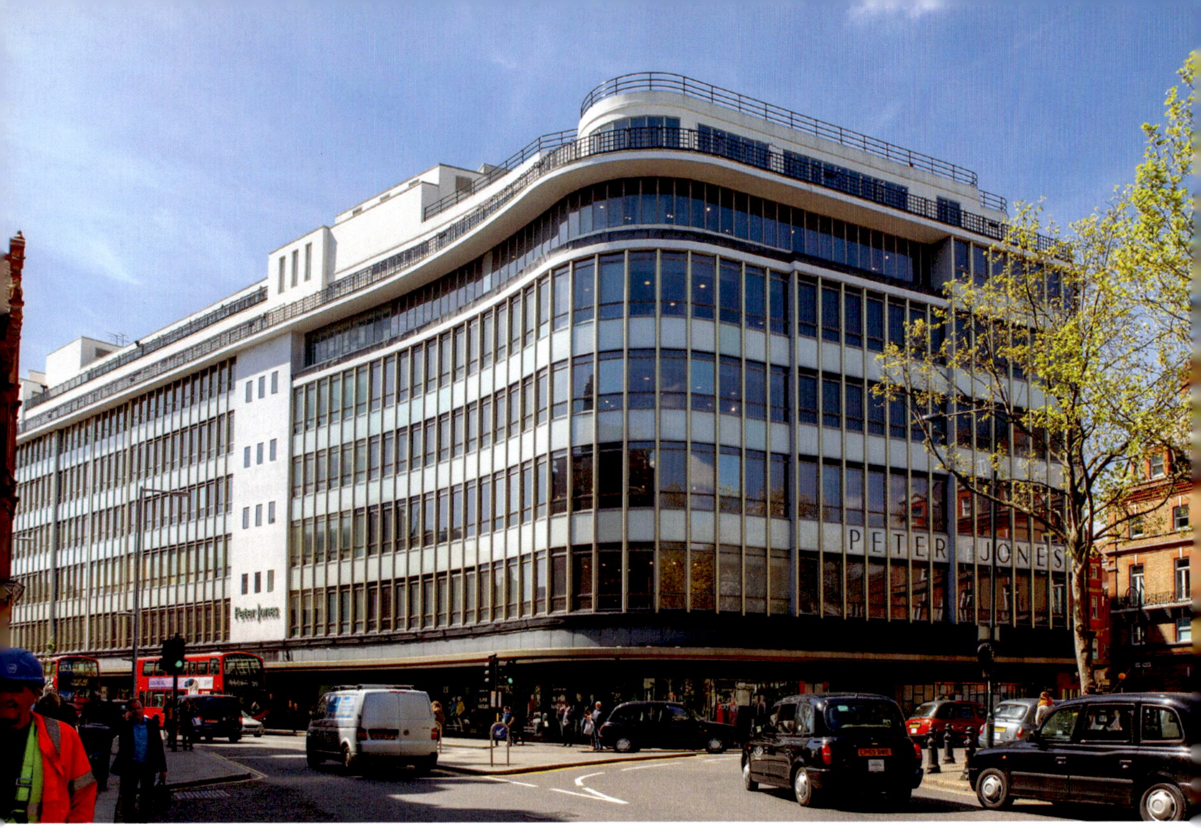

Peter Jones department store.

and remains very elegant. Occupying the entire west side of Sloane Square the building has not lost its appeal despite almost being one hundred years old. A major refurbishment in the early 2000s has made the shop interior both lighter and more spacious and unsurprisingly Peter Jones remains the favourite local corner shop for many Chelsea residents.

www.johnlewis.com

30. Flood Street Studios: Nos 1–11 and No. 72 Flood Street, SW3

Flood Street contains some superb examples of working studios used first by artists and later by photographers, sculptors and writers too. From the late 1860s speculative studio development began in Camden and then as the idea caught on similar studios were built in areas such as St John's Wood, Hampstead, Kensington and in Chelsea during the 1880s and 1890s.

Chelsea Manor Studios at Nos 1–11 Flood Street opened slightly later in 1902, and it was here at Michael Coopers Photographic Studio on 30 March 1967 that the legendary rock band the Beatles arranged a photo session to shoot the cover for their *Sgt. Pepper's Lonely Hearts Club Band* album. The cover image, masterminded by Jann Haworth and Peter Blake, featured the four group members

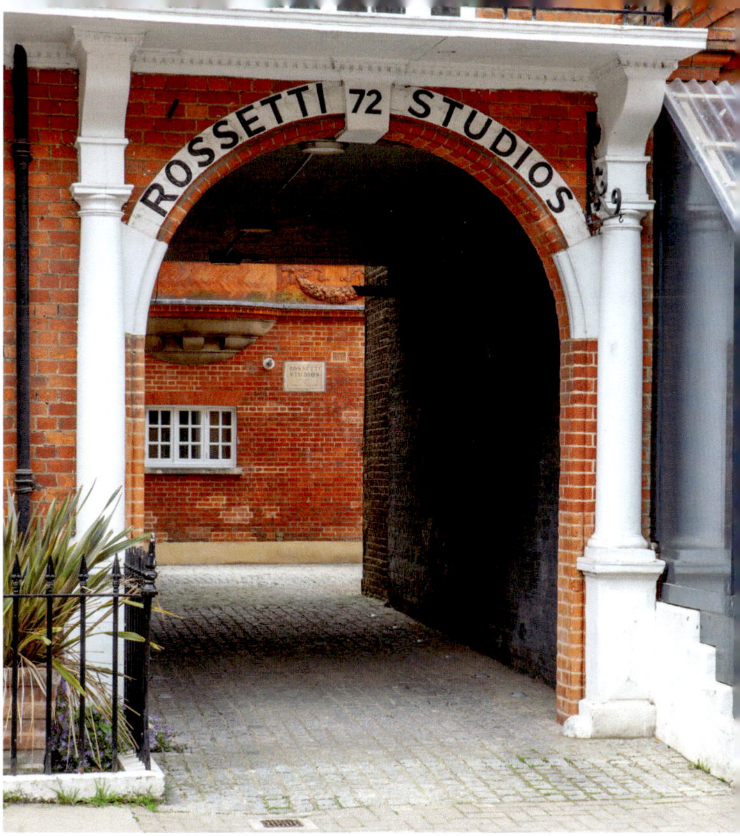

Right and below: Rossetti Studios.

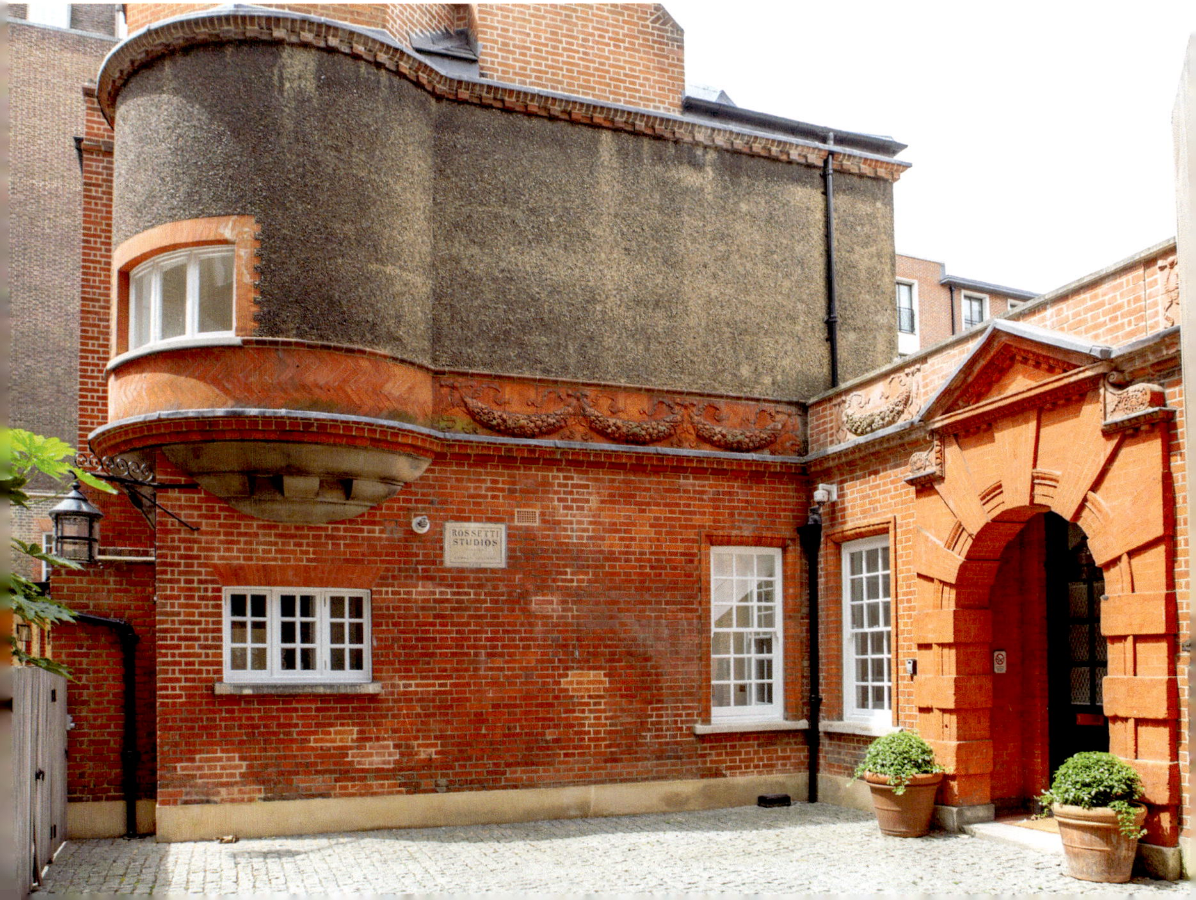

along with sixty-six celebrities in photographic and waxwork form. This resulted in a highly colourful collage and included names such as Mae West, Bob Dylan, Fred Astaire, Marlene Dietrich and Oscar Wilde. Although some of the studios are still used by designers and artists (both Graham Sutherland and Norman Parkinson have worked from here), others have been converted into apartments. In fact, the studio used by the Beatles was recently on the market as a two-bed apartment for over a million pounds.

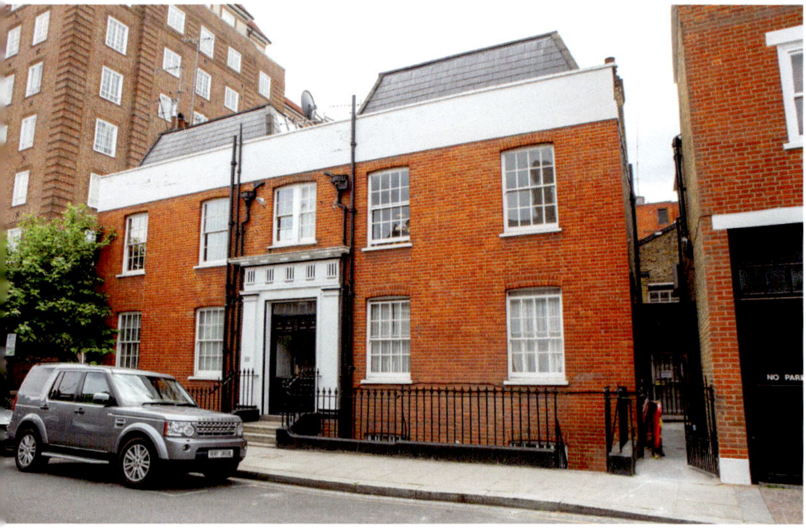

Left and below: Chelsea Manor Studios.

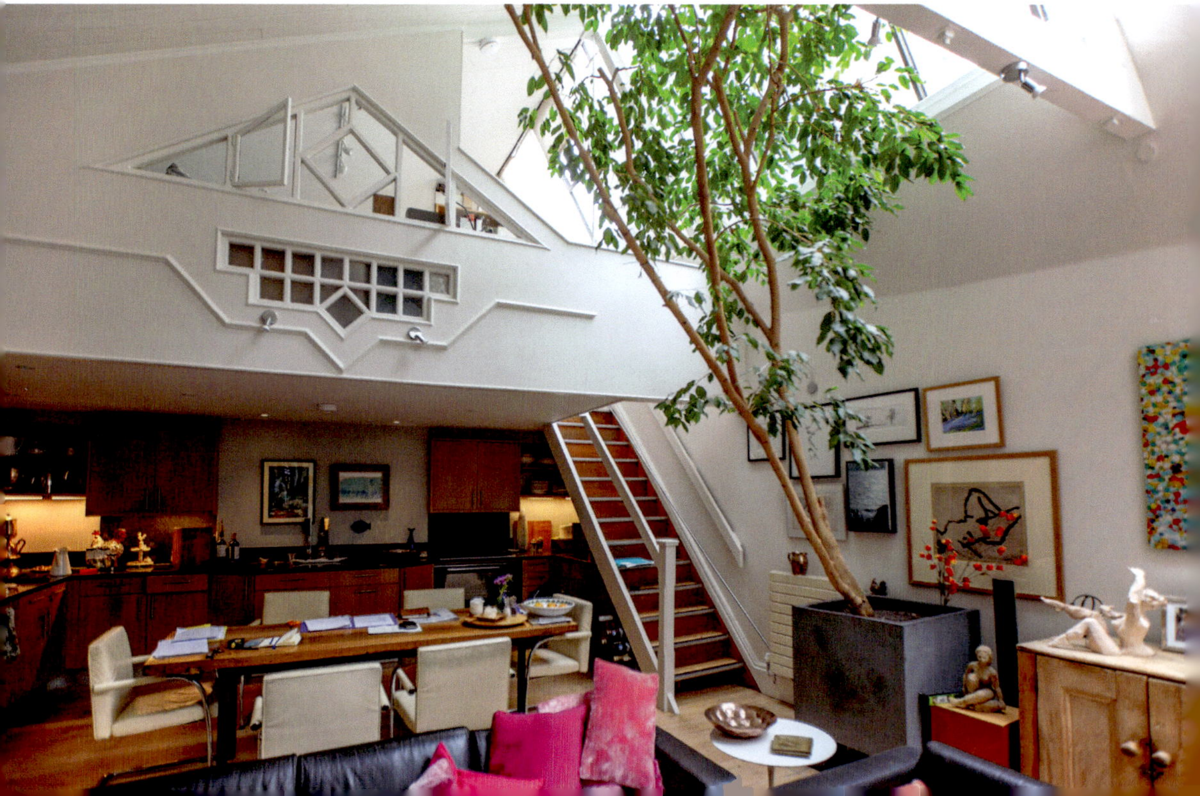

Further along the street you reach an archway beside Rossetti Garden Mansions which leads to the Rossetti Studios at No. 72. Built in the 1890s in the Queen Anne style in red brick and terracotta, they too were a speculative build as multiple artists' studios and still remain remarkably intact. In addition to their architectural and historic merit, they contain rare features such as slit doors giving access for canvases, galleries for storing canvases, living accommodation and changing rooms. The complex consists of four single-storey artists' studios and three studios two-storeys high. In the early 1900s artists Augustus John's and William Orpen's Chelsea Art School opened in Studios 4 and 5, and later the fashion photographer Ronald Traeger and theatre director George Devine worked here. The Cadogan Estate is responsible for Rossetti Studios' recent restoration which has enhanced the studios' character and has returned them to their original purpose and splendour.

www.cadogan.co.uk

31. Church of Our Most Holy Redeemer and St Thomas More, Upper Cheyne Row, SW3

Located at the junction of Cheyne Row and Upper Cheyne Row, it is impossible to miss this fine-looking Roman Catholic church. Considerably taller than the terraces it stands besides, it is Renaissance in style, mainly built of red brick and has a grand stone porch embellished with columns, above which is a broken curved pediment. On either side of the entrance are roundel windows that are surrounded by stonework and filled with stained glass depicting the saints Thomas More and Francis of Assisi. On opening in 1895 the church was known as the Church of Our Most Holy Redeemer. Forty years later, after the canonisation of Thomas More, its name was altered to include the saint's name and Thomas More's coat of arms was subsequently placed above the entrance.

As you enter inside the church there is a beautiful iron grille screen that separates the narthex from the nave. Decorated in pastel colours, the interior appears very light and airy and the nave and sanctuary are characterised by arcades and huge Ionic pilasters that support the panelled ceiling. During the Second World War the church was hit by a bomb and nineteen people taking shelter in the crypt sadly lost their lives. The bomb also destroyed the west wall and organ. Restoration was carried out in the post-war years and today Our Most Holy Redeemer Church carries Grade II listed status.

Where the church now stands is where the artist and potter, William de Morgan started his first pottery at the Orange House in the early 1870s. De Morgan was closely associated with the Arts and Crafts Movement and although he had begun his career working in the field of stained glass his focus changed to ceramics production when he moved to Chelsea. An innovator and perfectionist he is credited with having reintroduced the Renaissance technique of lustre

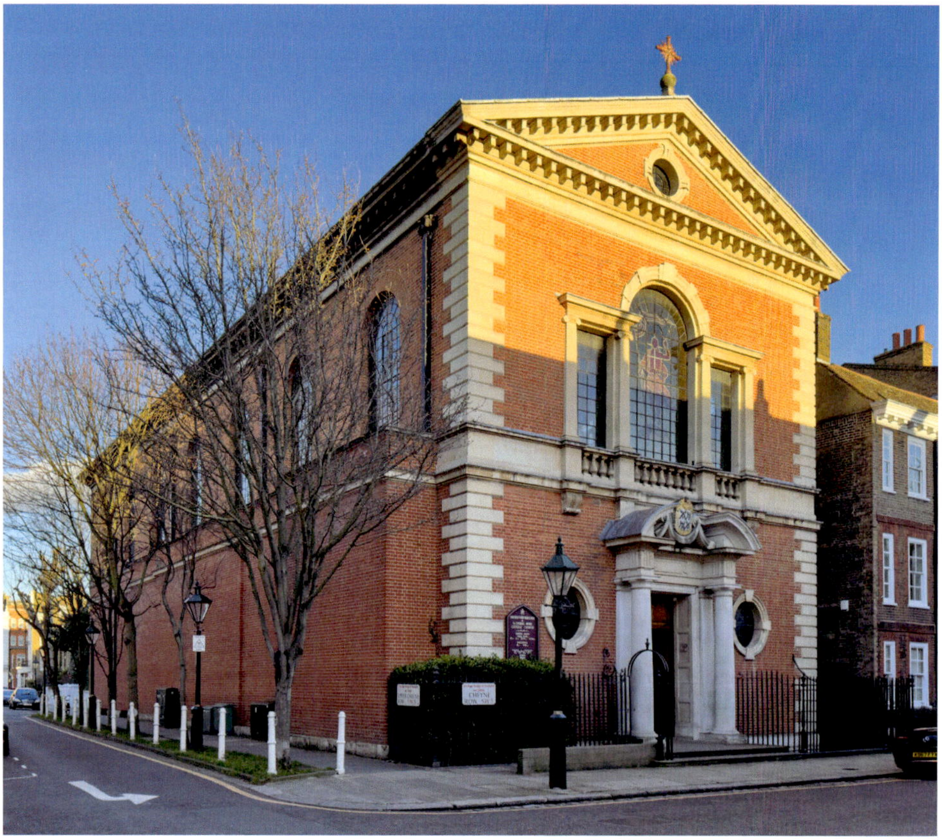

Above and below: Church of Our Most Holy Redeemer and St Thomas More.

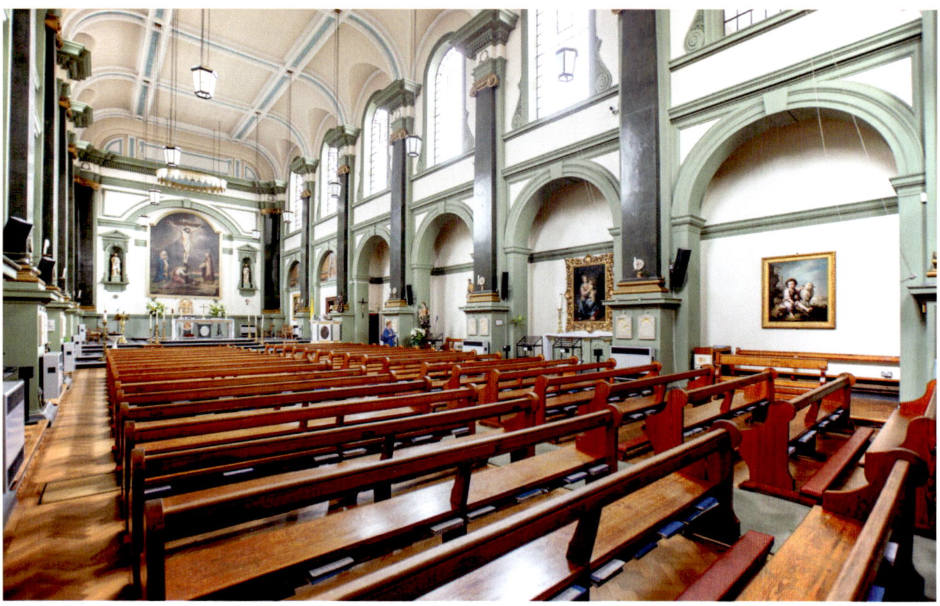

glazing in Britain. His work was greatly influenced by the Iznik pottery of the Ottoman Empire and by medieval designs which are frequently in evidence on his ceramic tiles, that were used by the Victorians in bathrooms, kitchens and fireplaces.

https://rcdow.org.uk

32. World's End and the World's End Estate, King's Road, SW3

World's End was probably so named because of its distance and perilous journey from London. Its inn, established by the 1660s was a tavern known particularly for its large grounds and tea gardens, described in Congreve's comedy *Love for Love* (1695) as 'a place of questionable reputation to the west of London'. Nonetheless, situated by the Thames and in such a rural spot surrounded by fields and market

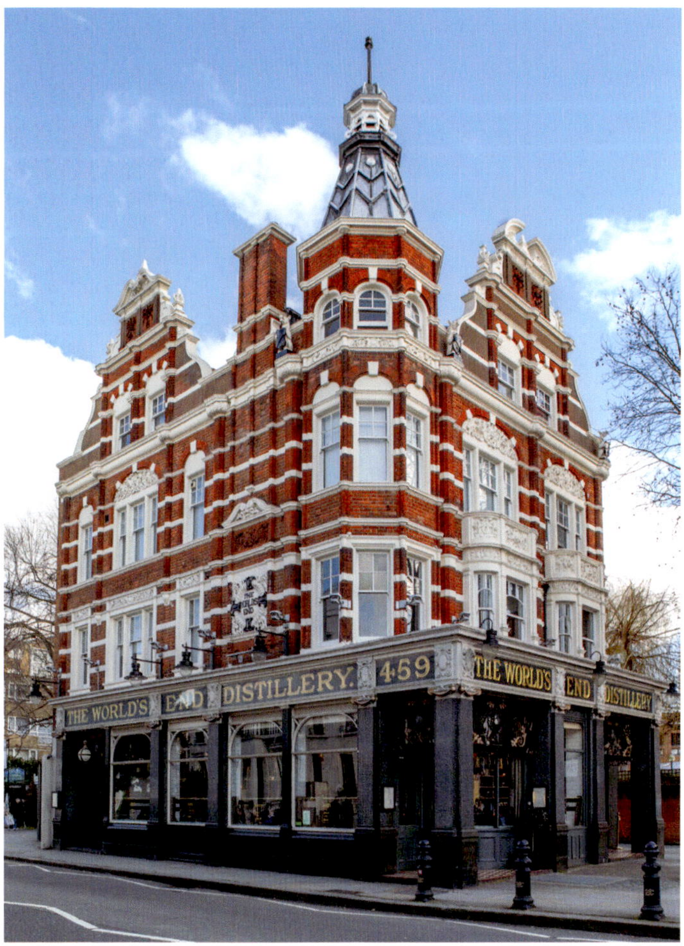

Former World's End pub.

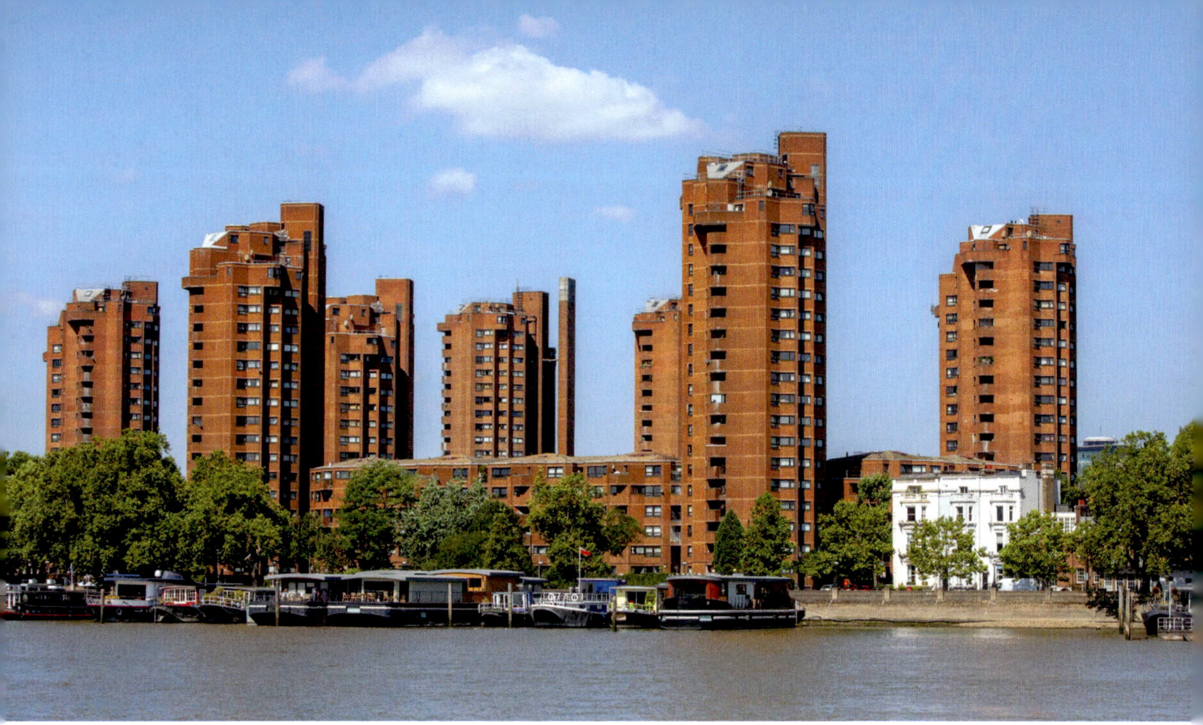

World's End estate.

gardens, visitors happily travelled here on pleasure boats to enjoy the entertainments on offer. The original pub was replaced in 1897 by the splendid Victorian building that exists today. Built in the Free Flemish Revival style in red brick with stone and banding (sometimes referred to as 'blood and bandages') it bears similarities to many of Chelsea's buildings of the period. A typical Victorian gin palace, the pub is highly decorated on its front with carved reliefs, gables, and turrets. Unfortunately, it has recently ceased trading and now stands, somewhat forlornly, in front of the borough's brutalist 1960s housing project, the World's End Estate.

Complementing the pub with its red-brown brick cladding, the estate consists of a group of polygonal towers and interlinking low-rise walkway blocks set in a figure of eight. Architects Eric Lyons and Jim Cadbury-Brown were responsible for the high-rise blocks' many-sided design, which gives them such a distinctive appearance. The estate is regarded as one of the most successful high-density council housing schemes of its time.

33. The Ivy Chelsea Garden, No. 197 King's Road, SW3

Formerly the site of the Six Bells public house, this Grade II listed building today houses the Ivy Chelsea Garden restaurant, part of the Troia Restaurant Group's Ivy Collection. The original inn (dating to 1722) was renowned for its exceptionally large bowling green and it was this space that was used by the new owners in 2014 to create a fabulous outdoor dining area. The garden has been utterly transformed and contains magnificent displays of wisteria and climbing roses on its pergolas as

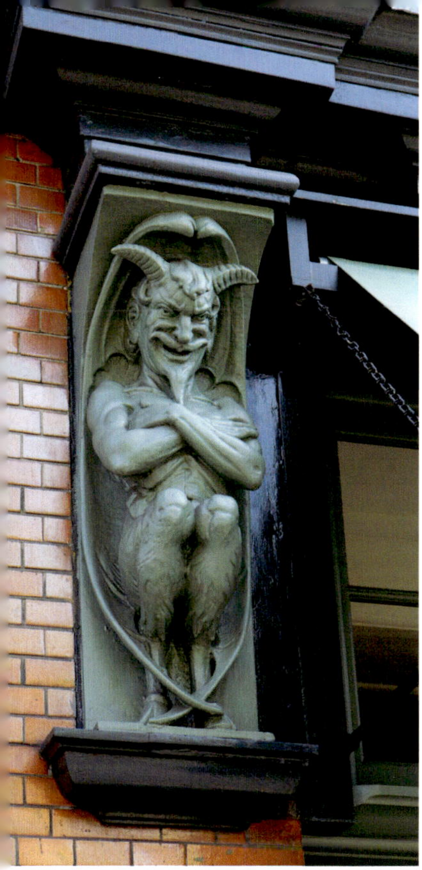

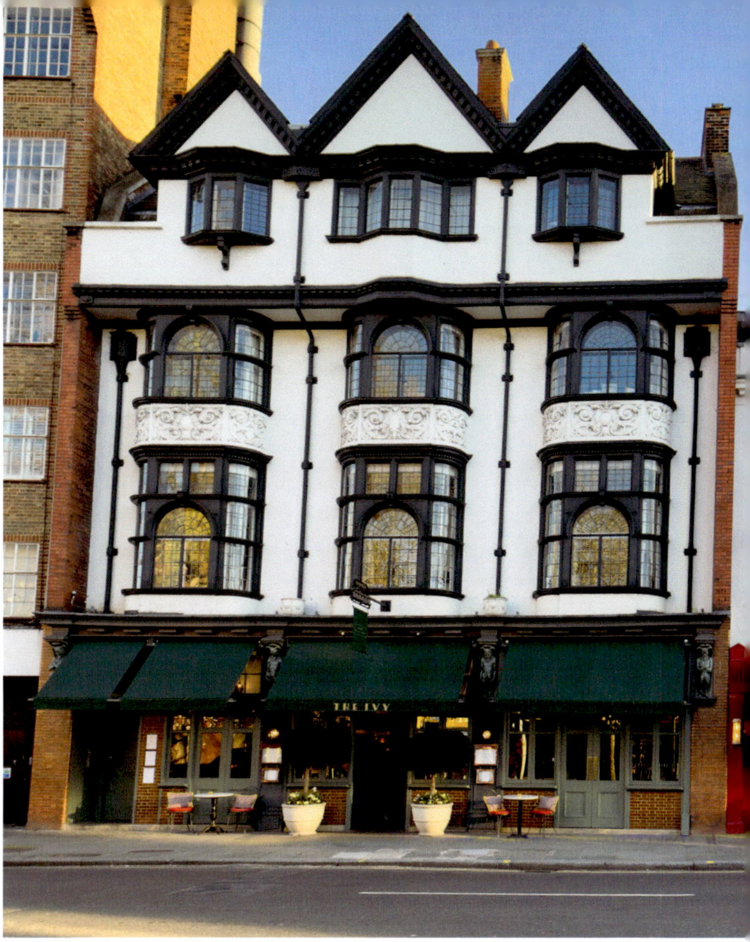

Above and right: The Ivy Chelsea Garden.

well as a great selection of brightly coloured flowers and plants around the open and covered seating areas. The interior is equally eye-catching with floral painted walls and a variety of seating scattered around the premises.

Although on the same site as the original pub, the present building was completed in 1900 when it was rebuilt in the mock-Tudor style to the designs of the architect G. R. Crickmay. It is said to have been the haunt of artist Augustus John and in the 1930s of the writers Dylan Thomas and Samuel Beckett. In the 1950s and 1960s it became a popular jazz venue, but from the 1980s until 2013 it was a pub with an American restaurant and known as 'Henry J. Beans public house'.

www.ivycollection.com

34. Cadogan Hall, No. 5 Sloane Terrace, SW1

When crossing Sloane Square into Cliveden Place be sure to look left to catch your first glimpse of Cadogan Hall. The building you see is made of Portland stone ashlar and quite unlike any other nearby. Indeed, its majestic tall tower topped with a dome-capped octagonal cupola makes you wonder if you are looking at a church or perhaps a mosque. Walk around the building (it sits between Sloane Terrace and Wilbraham Place) to marvel at its most original architecture, consisting of a graceful, covered arcade, pillars and round-arched windows – sometimes described as Byzantine Revival style or Free Byzantine with Asian touches. Its architect, R. F. Chisholm, having worked in India for many years, was obviously influenced by eastern culture and seems to have drawn his inspiration from the Byzantine, Romanesque and Islamic architectural styles. He designed the building early in the twentieth century for the First Church of Christ Scientist (CCS) an American church that had been set up in Boston, Massachusetts, by Mary Baker Eddy in 1879. The movement credited the Bible with mystic powers to heal the body and the mind and its motto declared: 'Heal the sick, raise the dead, cleanse the lepers, cast out demons'. The church in Chelsea was built as a response to the increasing popularity of the CCS and remained in use until 1996 when the congregation had significantly diminished.

Since 2004 the former church has been converted for use as a music and events space by the Cadogan Estate, who bought the building to safeguard its future.

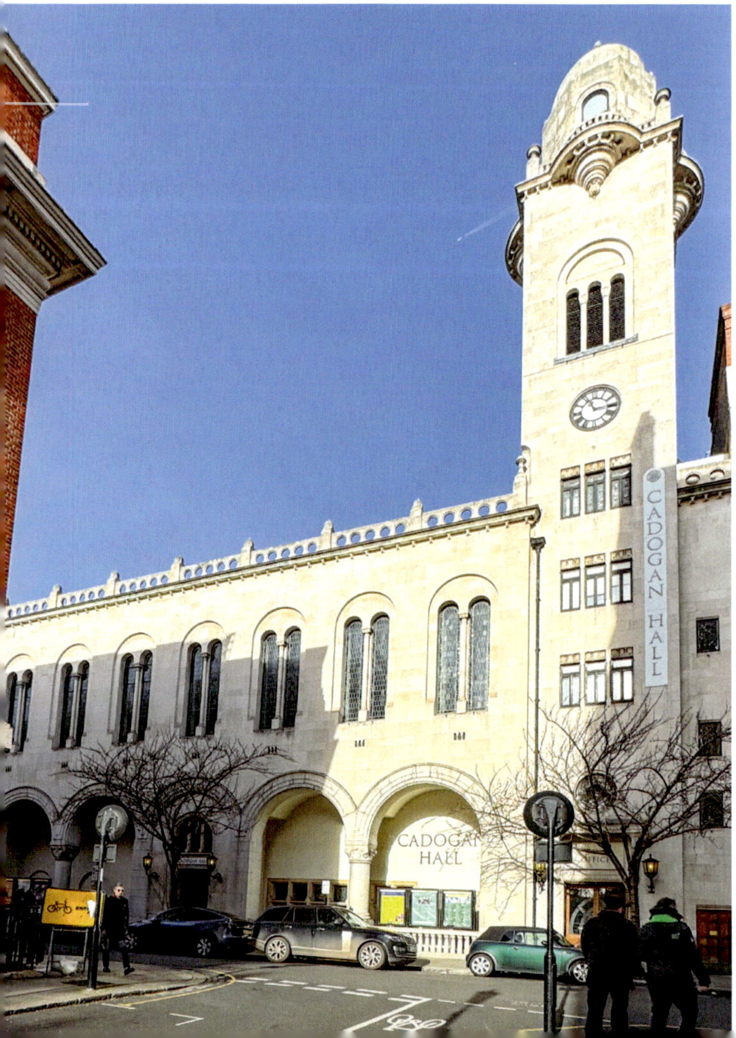

Left and below: Cadogan Hall.

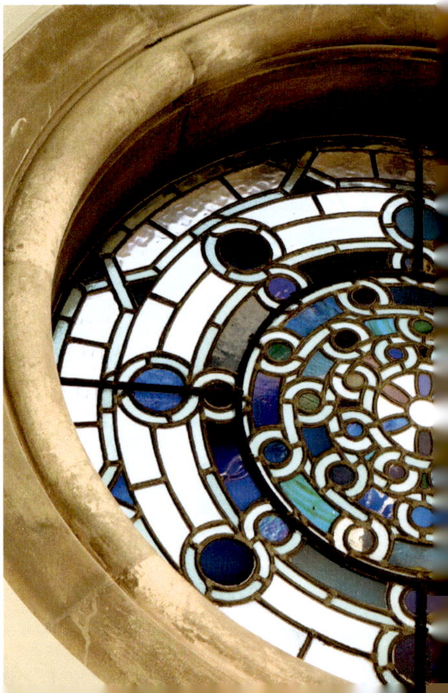

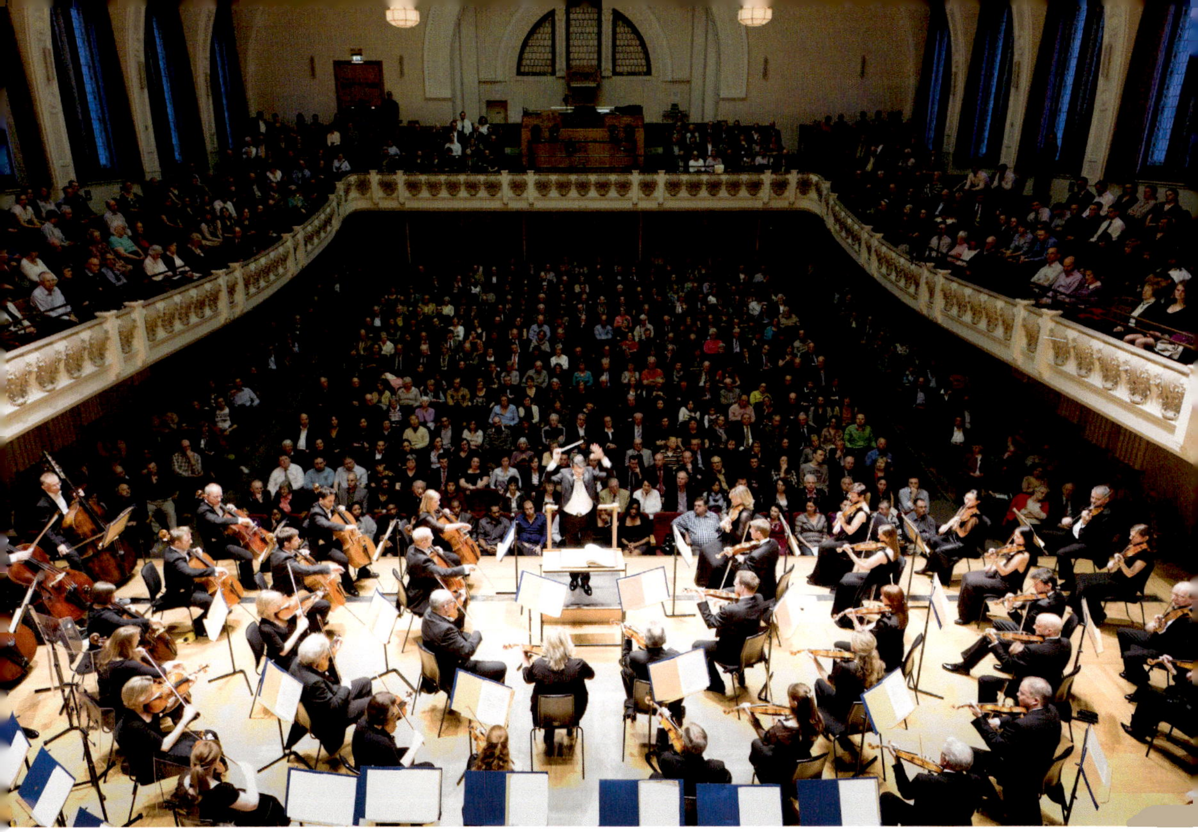

Cadogan Hall. (© Alex MacNaughton)

They instigated a major refurbishment which resulted in the introduction of state-of-the-art lighting and sound systems to the auditorium and made major improvements to the acoustics in the performance space. The wonderful stained-glass windows by Baron Arild Rosenkrantz have been restored and the seating has been made more comfortable. Cadogan Hall is now the permanent home of the Royal Philharmonic Orchestra and frequently hosts touring orchestras from across the world. It has become one of London's most successful venues with a wide programme of jazz, classical and folk music as well as interesting debates and conferences.

www.cadoganhall.com

35. Nos 46 and 46c Old Church Street and No. 69 King's Road

Wright's Dairy opened on Cook's Ground (today's Glebe Place) in 1796 at a time when Chelsea was full of farms, market gardens and orchards. As the Industrial Revolution took hold in London the small village became more and more populated, new streets and houses were erected and naturally all food, especially milk and dairy products, fruit, vegetables and cereals were in great demand. The dairy had a thriving business and kept about fifty cows on its farm. These were put out to graze on pasture in the fields behind the dairy buildings close to the area we now know as Old Church Street. Almost a century later as urbanisation struck, and buildings replaced former fields the dairy was forced to move slightly west into premises in Old Church Street. Today, Wright's Dairy's premises at No. 46 are easily recognised by the sculpture of a cow's head that sits between its windows on the second floor. There are also several colourful wall tiles at ground-floor level that remind us of the dairy's rural past: scenes in which a milkmaid is painted with a wooden pail on her head and one titled 'an early mower' of a man drinking from a barrel while holding a scythe in his hand. To the side of No. 46 is a courtyard building set back from the road which was once part of the dairy. It too bears a cow's head on its façade and an inscription 'Estd.1796' on either side of the cow's head.

Wright's Dairy also had a shop on the corner of Smith Street and the King's Road where a further cow's head sculpture juts out beneath the top of the corner turret.

In the 1950s Wright's was bought out by another dairy group and in 1964 its buildings were transformed by two young enthusiastic sound engineers into

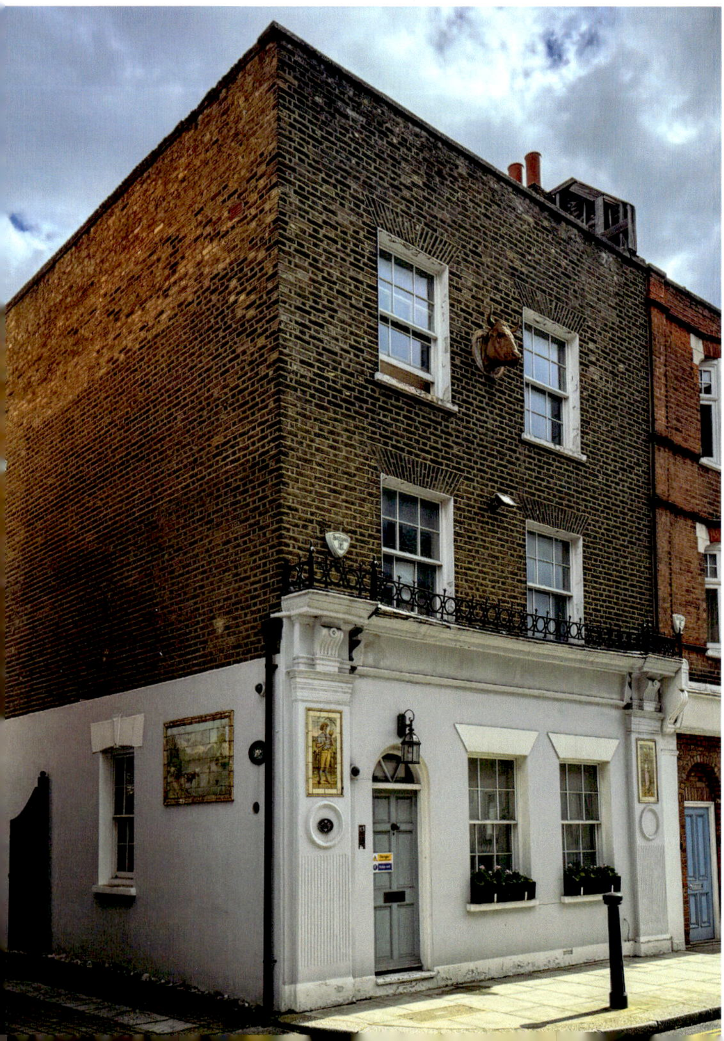

Left and below: No. 46c Old Church Street.

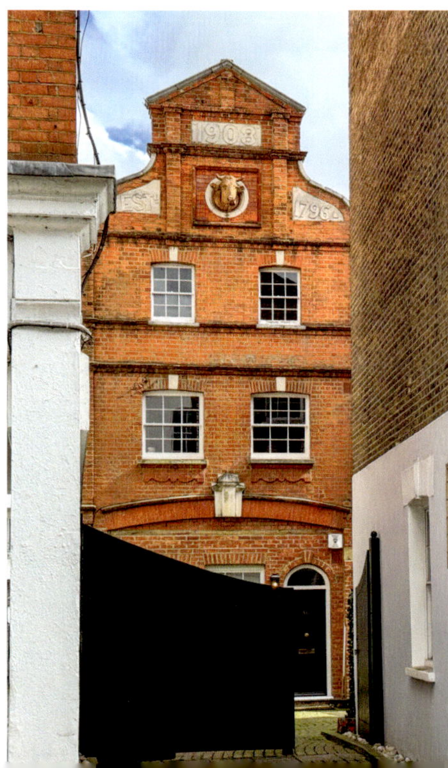

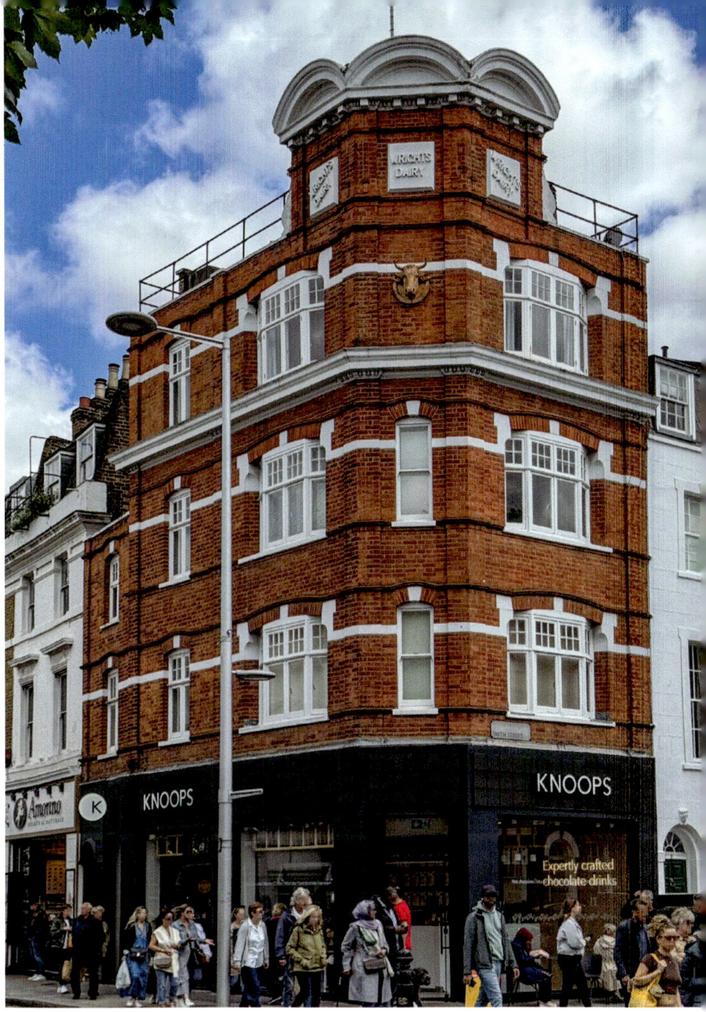

No. 69 King's Road.

a recording studio, Sound Techniques Ltd. The studio was extremely successful and many of the greatest bands and singers of the 1960s and 1970s recorded their albums here, including Alice Cooper, the Animals, the Beatles, David Bowie, T-Rex and Elton John amongst others.

36. Michelin House, No. 81 Fulham Road, SW3

An outstanding building for its colour, decoration and iconic style, Michelin House is a definite landmark on the Fulham Road. It was built between 1909 and 1911 as the UK headquarters and tyre warehouse for the Michelin Tyre Company Ltd of France, and was built as part of the company's expansion across the Channel. Michelin was one of the early pioneers in this country to use the system of ferro-concrete construction, which allowed for a spacious building interior without the need for supporting columns and had the additional benefit of being fire-resistant – an absolute 'must' in a building containing 30,000 rubber tyres. The ground floor was given over to fitting bays to service the cars of passing motorists, whilst the

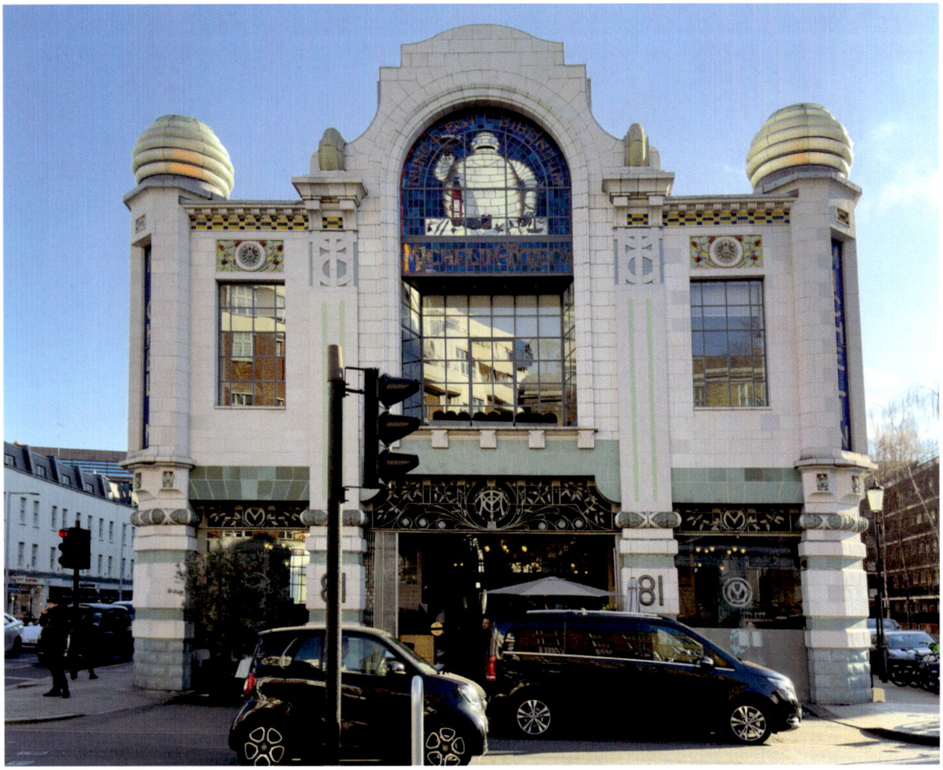

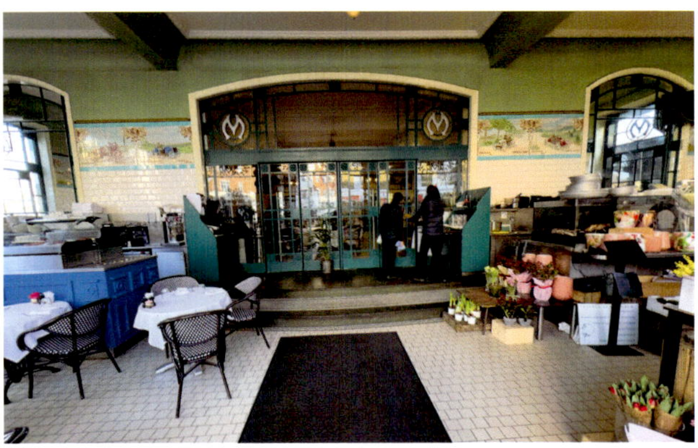

Above and left: Michelin House.

basement beneath stored the tyres that were delivered upstairs in a lift. There was also a 'Touring Office' with maps for motorists to plan their journeys and offices on the higher floors for head office staff.

Michelin House was designed by a company engineer Francois Espinasse, in the art nouveau and early art deco styles. It has many references in its external windows and within the building to 'Bibendum' the Michelin Man, who has always been the advertising face of the company. He is emblazoned in the stunning stained-glass windows above the main entrance and as part of the mosaic on the ground floor. Exquisite ceramic tiles displaying pictures of famous racing cars adorn Michelin

House's ground floor and its external walls while at the upper corner of the building's façade there are imposing glass pinnacles that represent stacked tyres.

Michelin closed its premises here in the 1980s and the building was then bought up by the restaurateur and retailer Sir Terence Conran and the publisher Paul Hamlyn. They undertook a major refurbishment, restoring some of the building's lost features and converted it into a restaurant, a bar, shop and offices. Nowadays Michelin House incorporates office space, an upstairs restaurant, Bosi at Bibendum, and an oyster bar at street level. At night the building lights up the Fulham Road and continues to delight passers-by with its beauty as well as the clever use of art and design to advertise a major brand.

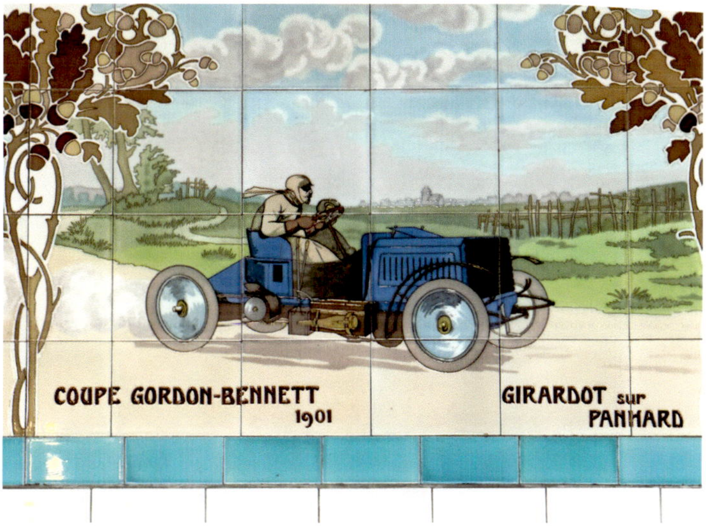

Right: Wall panel within Michelin House.

Below: Michelin House.

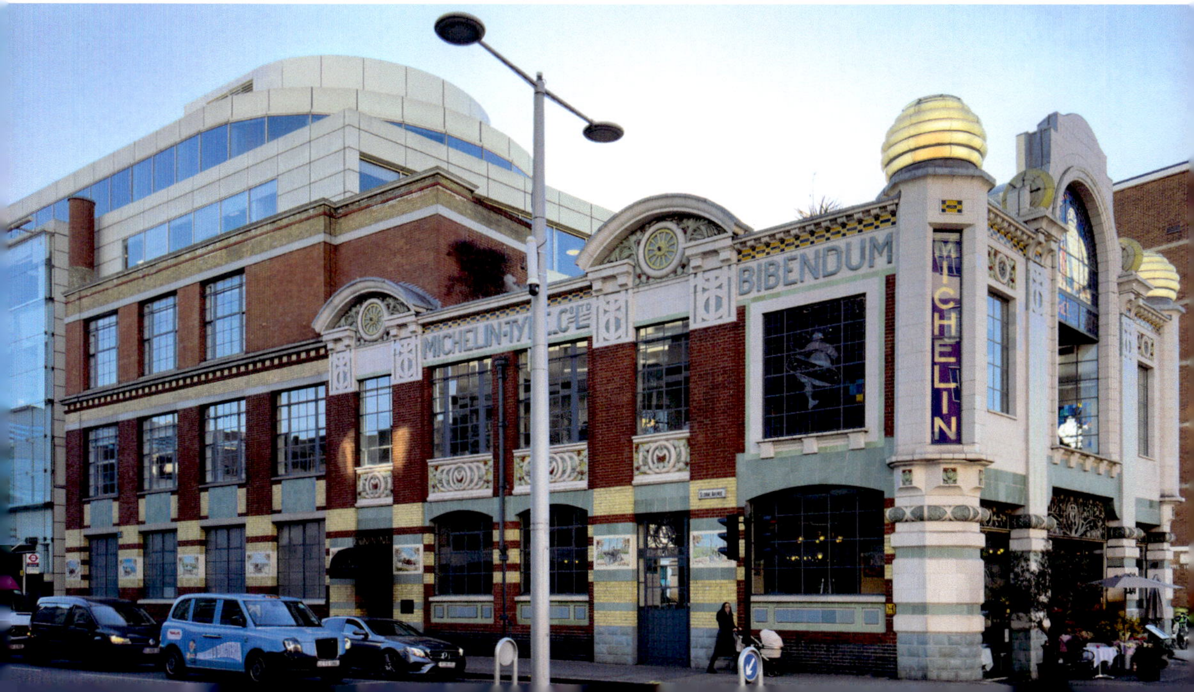

37. Samuel Lewis and Sutton Trust Estates, Ixworth Place, SW3

These two handsome and sturdily built social housing estates occupy much of the area in and around Ixworth Place. They were built within several years of each other in the early twentieth century. The Sutton Model Dwellings (as they were originally called) were completed in 1913 while the Samuel Lewis Trust for Dwellings for the Poor opened two years later in 2015. Both estates owe their existence to the philanthropy of wealthy benefactors who saw and understood the plight of the decent poor in Chelsea and felt the need to provide well-built, sanitary homes for them at affordable rents.

When the investor William Sutton (1833–1900) died he left much of his fortune to provide quality housing for the poor. The Chelsea Estate, made to accommodate 2,200 people, was built five storeys high in red brick and terracotta with high chimneys. Although quite uniform in character, the blocks are separated by courtyards and communal spaces and the buildings display attractive features such as curved stone pediments above the entrance porches and black railings.

The Samuel Lewis Trust Dwellings similarly came about due to the bequest of a rich financier, Samuel Lewis (1837–1901). The estate, like the Sutton Model

Samuel Lewis Trust Dwellings.

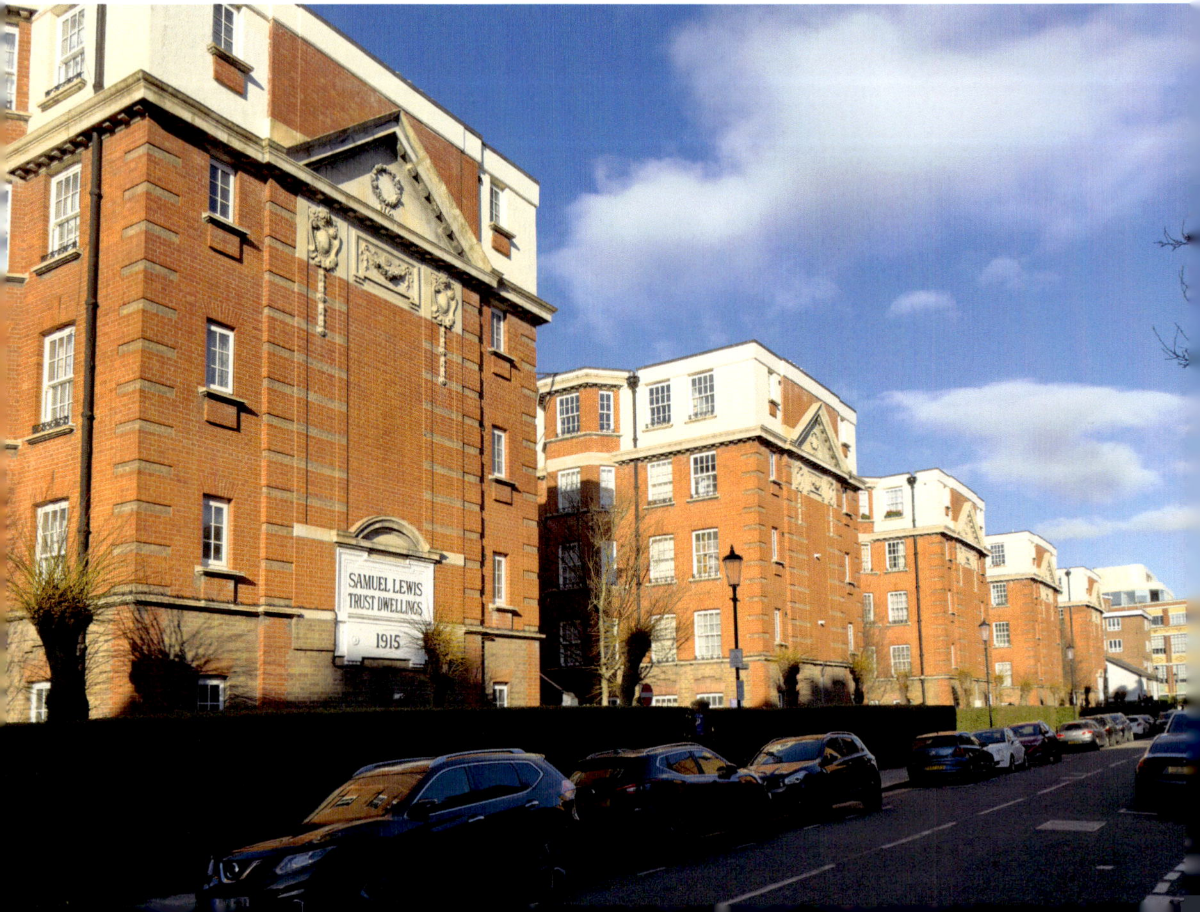

Dwellings, comprises a string of blocks interspersed by courtyards and landscaped areas. Mainly built in red brick and stone with yellow stock brick at ground level, the buildings are embellished with stone reliefs on their exterior façades. Unsurprisingly, the appearance of both estates fits in well with the Queen Anne Revival buildings elsewhere in the vicinity and although not perhaps as ornate as some in nearby squares, the homes are attractive and dominate the street scene.

In recent years the Sutton Estates' blocks came under threat of demolition due to their continuing deterioration. The estates' current owners, the housing association Affinity Sutton, proposed to reduce the number of dwellings and replace them with modern homes, but this sparked off such a strong campaign to save the historic and much-loved blocks that ultimately the proposals were dropped and instead of new buildings the estate is currently undergoing restoration and refurbishment.

38. Cabmen's Shelter, Chelsea Embankment, SW3

The green cabmen's shelter is a greatly loved part of London's transport heritage and the wooden huts are considered by many to be as iconic as the capital's red buses or black cabs. Only thirteen of the original sixty-one shelters have survived since they were first introduced in 1875 and the majority hold Grade II listed status.

Café Pier.

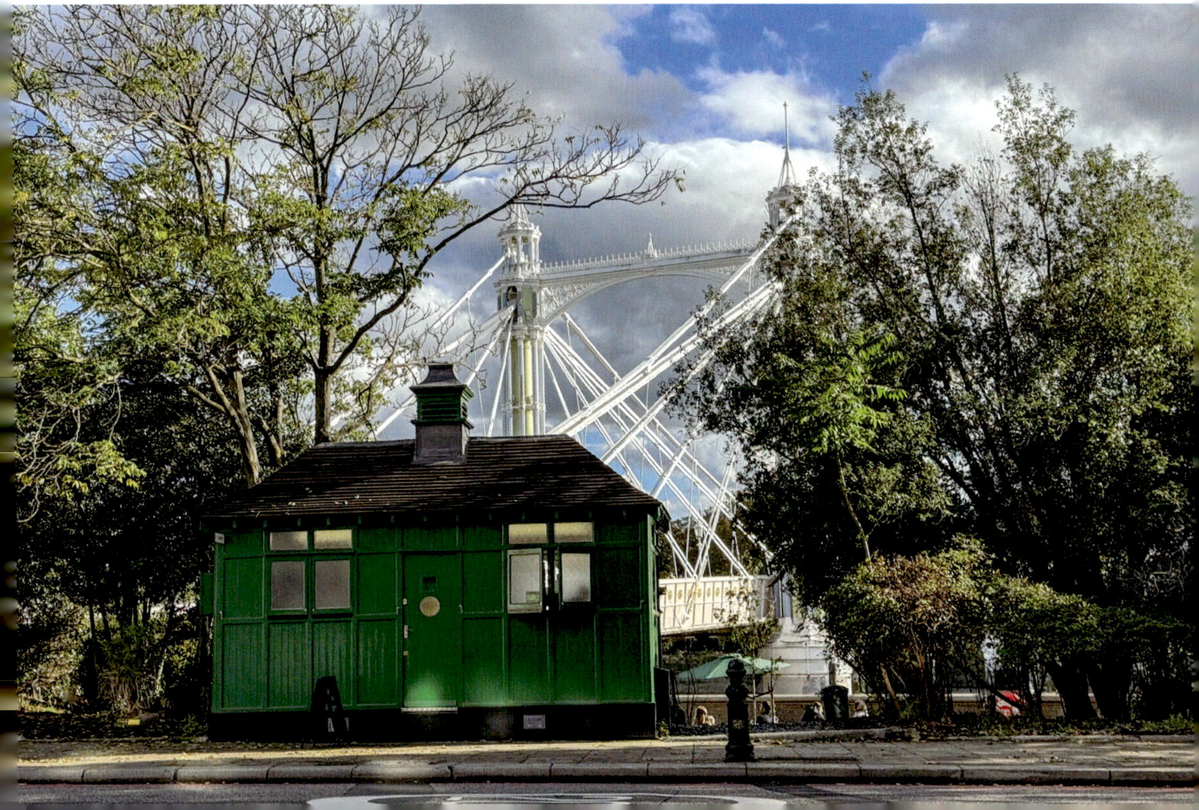

Easily recognised for their brightly painted green exterior, the shelters were conceived as a safe resting place for drivers of the Victorian hansom cabs. The nature of a cabman's work meant that he worked outside in all weathers, and prior to the construction of the shelters, cabmen would seek refuge in nearby pubs to get warm and dry. Many ended up the worse for wear having drunk too much alcohol, making them unfit to drive and furthermore making it difficult for customers to find a sober driver. As a result, the Cabmen's Shelter Fund (CSF) was formed in the 1870s to address the problem, led by the 7th Earl of Shaftesbury, MPs and other philanthropists.

The resultant shelters were of an identical size, conforming to rules of the Metropolitan Police, which stated that due to their position on the public highway they were to be no longer than a horse and cart. The CSF also laid down strict regulations that ensured only qualified cabbies could enter the huts and when inside they could eat and take refreshments but were forbidden to drink alcohol, gamble or swear.

The cabmen's shelter on Chelsea Embankment was one of the later models built in 1910 and sits right beside Albert Bridge. As the embankment is now a designated Red Route today's black cabs cannot stop on the road here, but the hut, which has recently undergone renovation, has since launched as a public facility – Café Pier, open Thursday to Sunday from 10 a.m. to 4 p.m.

Chelsea is fortunate in having two cabmen's shelters. The other one, dating to 1892, is found in Pont Street close to its junction with Sloane Street. Unlike Café Pier, it continues to serve London's cab drivers with refreshments and provides them with a place to meet colleagues.

39. Former Temperance Billiard Hall, Nos 131–141 King's Road, and Motorcar Garage, No. 15 Flood Street, SW3

The American ladies' clothing retailer Anthropologie now occupies this corner building, which was originally built as a Temperance Billiard Hall between 1912 and 1914. The temperance movement was keen to offer the working man a substitute to the public house, thus the hall bore many features in common with the grand gin palaces of the period, particularly in its use of stained glass, plasterwork, patterned tiles and attractive architecture. However, no liquor was sold on the premises and, like other temperance halls built in the early twentieth century, the emphasis was purely on recreational activities such as the popular game of billiards.

The hall today holds a Grade II listing which Historic England asserts it merits because it is 'a well-preserved example of one of the architecturally impressive early temperance billiard halls, now quite rare nationally' and is also due to its 'special architectural interest ... for the eclectic detailing, characterful Queen Anne style elevations and strong presence in the streetscape'. Certainly, the building

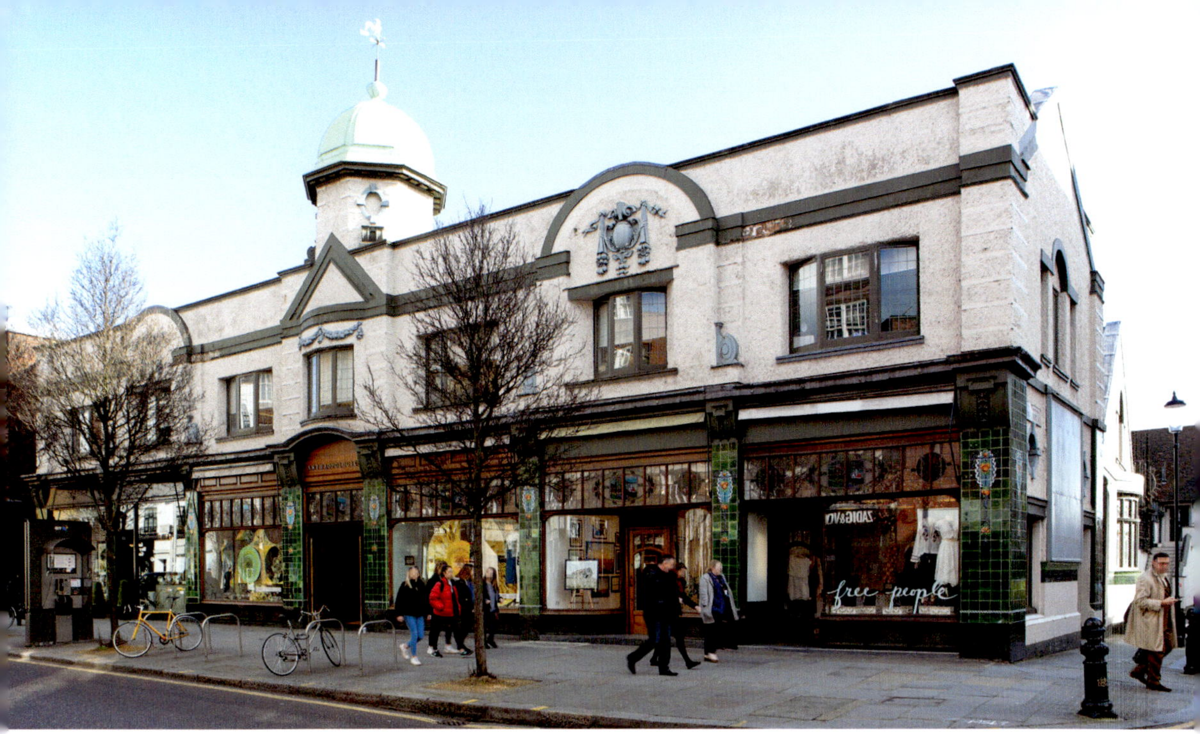

Above: Anthropologie, former Temperance Billiard Hall.

Below: Anthropologie, former motorcar garage.

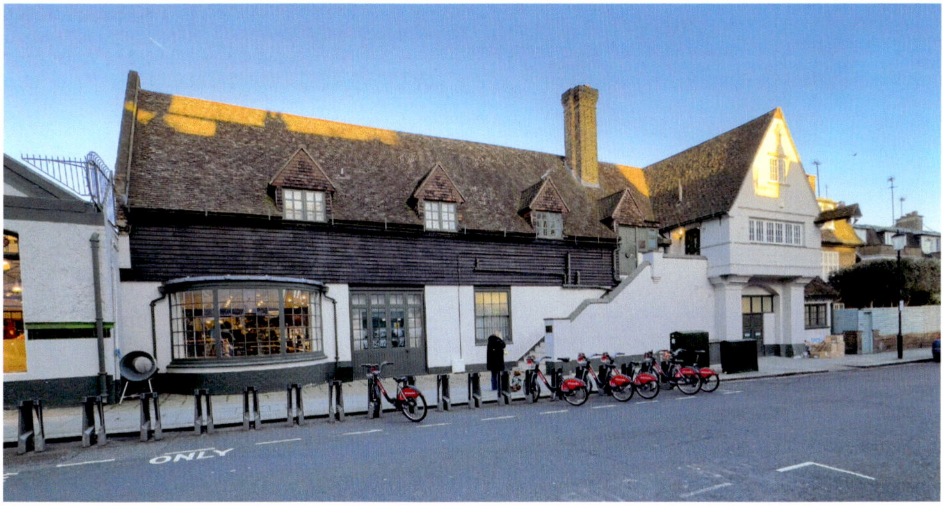

stands out on the King's Road for its deep green exterior tiling, art nouveau glass and green domed cupola above the store's main entrance.

The inside of the building too has retained many of its original features and displays art nouveau stained-glass skylights and an ornate metal truss roof. Nowadays, the shop connects with its neighbouring building in Flood Street, a further building of considerable interest and history. Built as a motorcar garage in 1919, its design in the Arts and Crafts style seems unusually traditional for a modern building of the time. Its steep-pitched tiled roof, weatherboarding and tall brick chimneys make it appear more like a rural home than a garage. Yet, the premises were specifically built as a mechanics garage and its primary role was car repair. Like the temperance hall, it holds Grade II status and is included on the National Heritage List due to its significance as a surviving structure from the interwar period, a time when motoring shifted from being purely fashionable (and available as a pastime for the wealthy) to a daily form of transport used by the masses.

40. The Bluebird Restaurant, No. 350, King's Road, SW3

Just a stone's throw away from the Flood Street garage is another tribute to the motor industry – today's Bluebird Restaurant. When the building first opened in 1923 it was Europe's greatest motorcar complex and had facilities to sell petrol and to service vehicles; it was so spacious that it could accommodate 300 cars in the main garage. The site also housed workshops, writing rooms for its patrons and lounges – one for ladies, the other for car owners and chauffeurs. Bluebird Garage was designed for the Bluebird Motor Company in the contemporary art deco style by the architect Robert Sharp and made with a steel frame and reinforced concrete. The garage with its stuccoed frontage was set back from the road and enclosed on either side by attractive four-storey (plus attic) red-brick residential blocks, one of which originally included chauffeurs' accommodation. The land speed record breaker, Major Malcolm Campbell, was associated with the garage for many

The Bluebird restaurant.

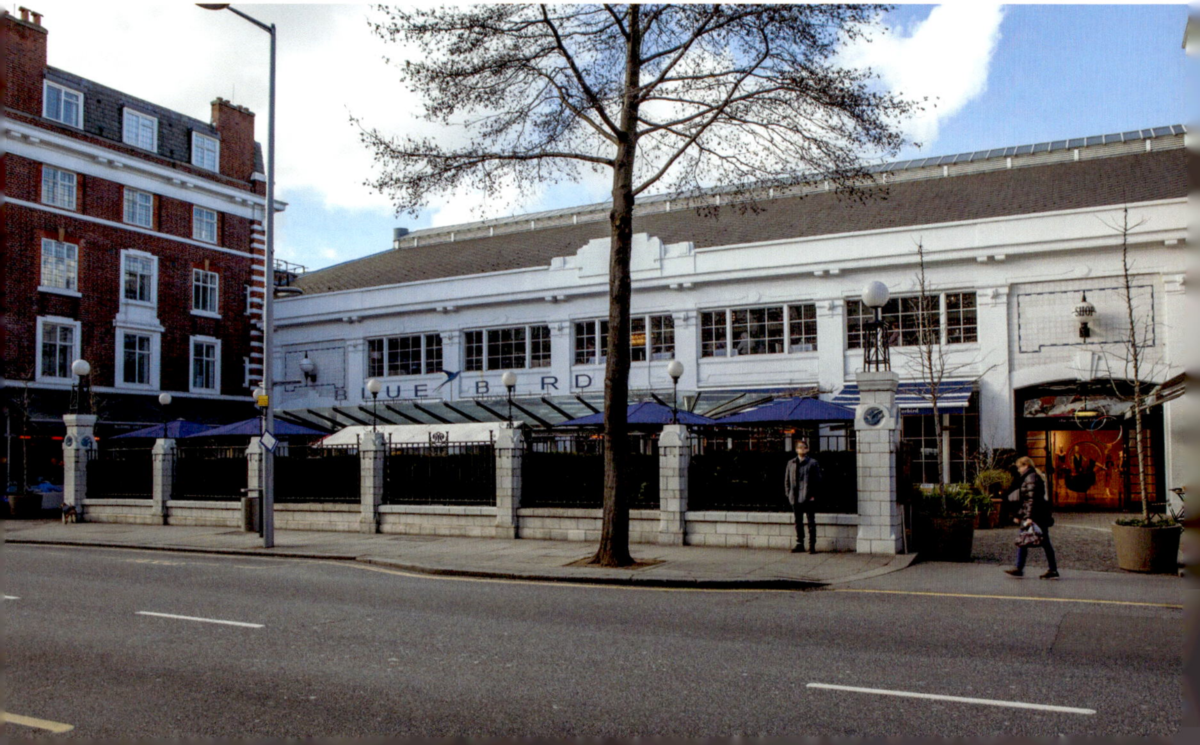

years and stored his racing cars here. Having won the world speed record on land many times, he then set the water speed record four times, his highest speed being achieved on Coniston Water in August 1939 in the Bluebird K4.

In the latter part of the twentieth century the building became known as Carlyle Garages and was used for a while by the Ambulance Service, but as the fabric of the former garage deteriorated it was converted for use as a retail and leisure space called 'Fashion Arena'. In 1997 Sir Terence Conran's Conran Group purchased the building, transforming it into the 'Bluebird Garstrodrome' consisting of a food-store, chef shop, restaurant, bar, café and private dining rooms.

The Bluebird changed direction again in 2006 when it came under the umbrella of D&D London, a group known for its great food, service and world-class design. D&D's diverse collection of restaurants and bars are found throughout London and the UK, and in New York and Paris. Bluebird's highly acclaimed restaurant and bar now occupies the first floor of the 1920s garage building whilst the excellent less-formal Bluebird Café is located in the courtyard facing the King's Road.

www.bluebird-restaurant.co.uk

41. Old Church Street, SW3

Apart from being one of Chelsea's oldest roads and lined with Georgian and Victorian housing, Old Church Street boasts one of the most (if not the most) expensive houses in Chelsea, two 1930s modernist houses and it is where the celebrated Chelsea Arts Club has been based since the early twentieth century.

Sloane House and its adjacent lodge sit near the King's Road and are owned by the heiress and socialite Petra Ecclestone. The property is said to contain Chelsea's largest private grounds and although the house has retained its historic Georgian exterior, the interior has been utterly transformed by its owner and now has a basement with an indoor pool, wellness rooms, a kid's playhouse, cinema and squash courts.

In total contrast, the pair of houses at Nos 66 and 64 are decidedly functional in appearance, built in concrete and lack external embellishment. The houses were designed in the mid-1930s by two sets of architects: No. 66, (Levy House) by the Bauhaus School founder, Walter Gropius and Maxwell Fry, while No. 64 (Cohen House) was built to the designs of Erich Mendelsohn and Serge Chermayeff. It is difficult to see Levy House clearly as it sits at a right angle to its neighbouring property (No. 64), which extends horizontally along the street making it seem more of an industrial than domestic building. Both houses are typical of the modernist style, endowed with an abundance of glass and concrete, curtain windows and flat roofs, and display minimal decoration. When the houses were built, they were the height of modernity, and they carry listed building status today as examples of excellent modernist architecture. No. 64 remains largely unchanged, but No. 66 has been altered greatly over the years.

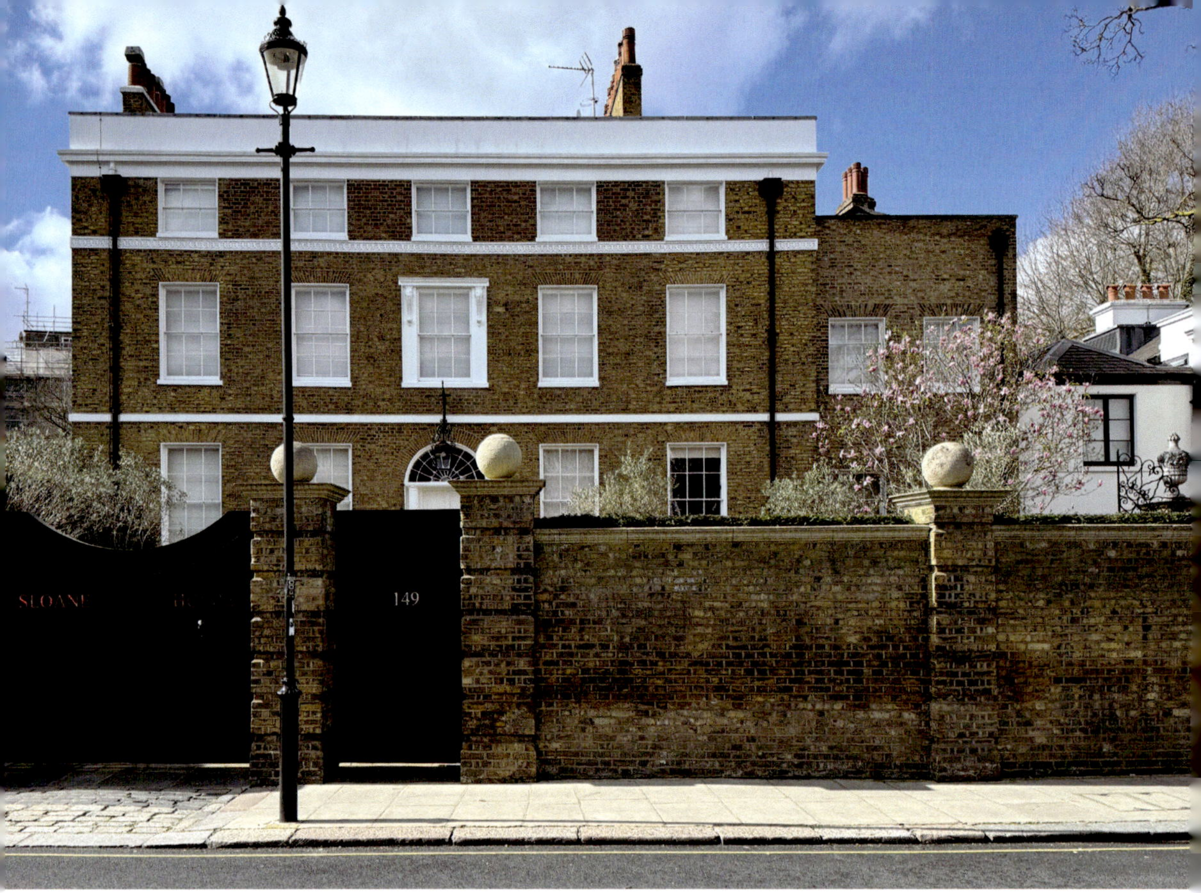

Above: Sloane House.

Below: Modernist houses, Old Church Street.

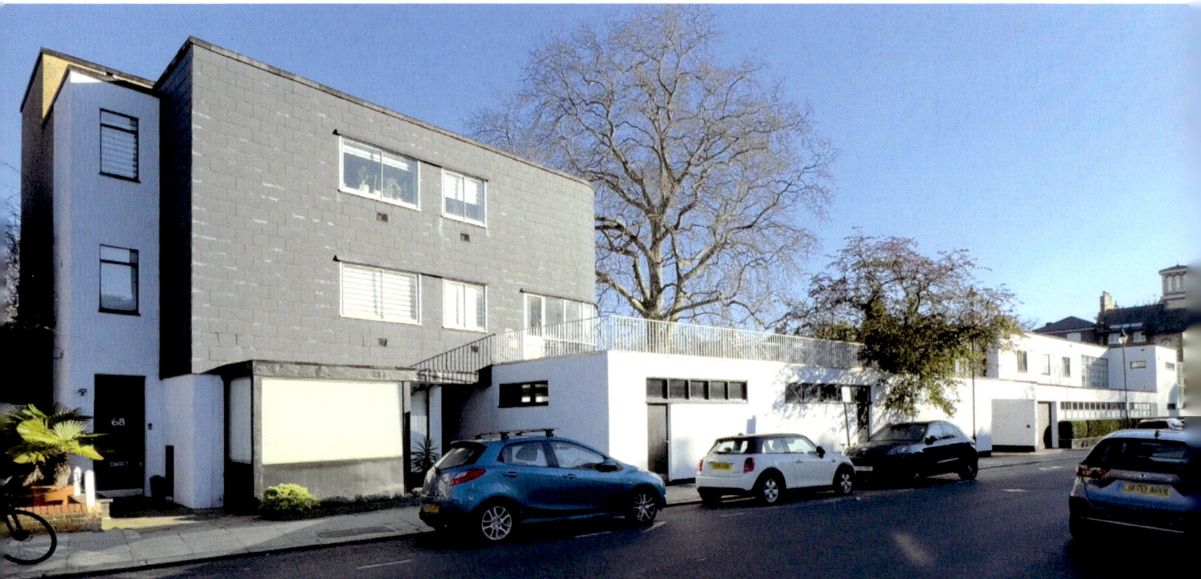

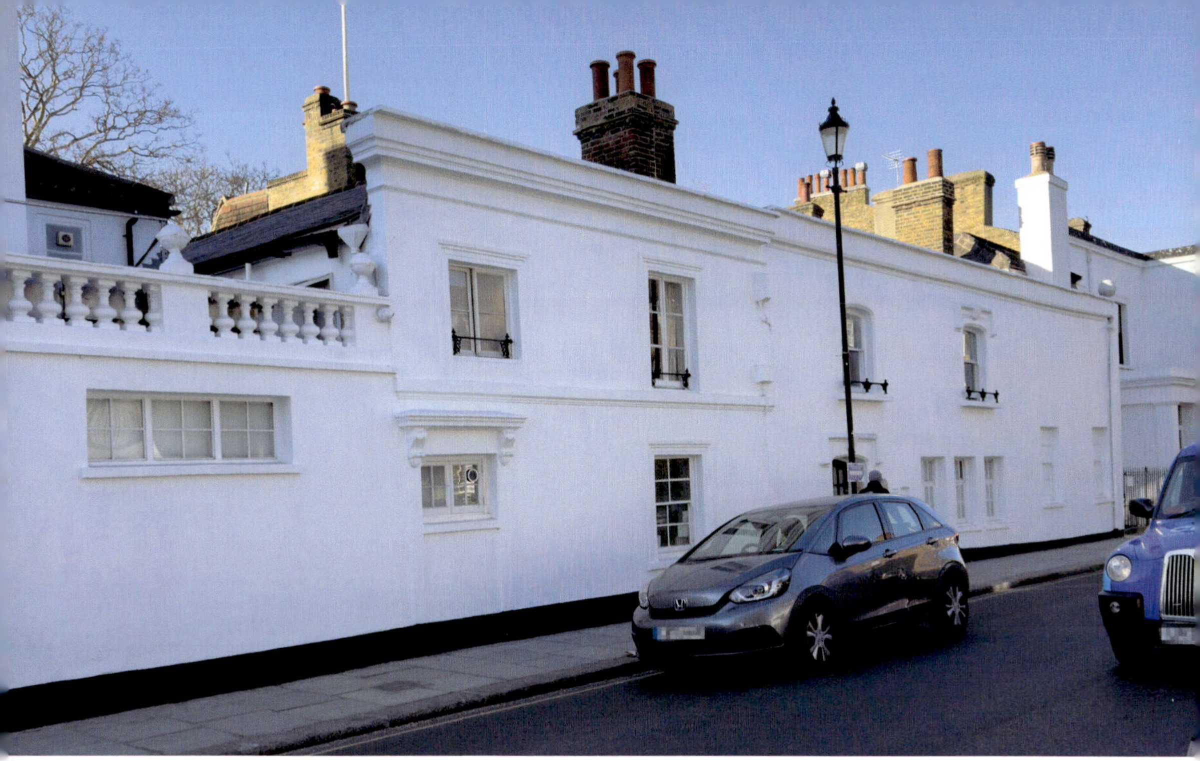

The Chelsea Arts Club.

Across the road at No. 143 is Chelsea Arts Club, instigated by the artist Whistler in the 1890s. It has always had a reputation for its wild New Year's Eve and Mardi Gras parties, which for fifty years were held at the Royal Albert Hall. Nowadays, themed parties of a bohemian nature take place in the club's Chelsea home and remain similarly lavish and raucous occasions.

42. National Army Museum, Royal Hospital Road, SW3

The National Army Museum (NAM), designed by William Holford & Partners in the post-war brutalist style, was established in 1961 and is the main authority on the history of the British Army. Since opening, the museum has formed a very large collection relating to the army's role, resulting in today's excellent and wide-ranging exhibits that describe its work at home and around the world. The NAM illustrates British military history from the English Civil War to the present day through its five galleries – Formation, Soldier, Global Role, Conflict in Europe and Army at Home. The Soldier Gallery explains what it is like to serve as a soldier in the UK and abroad and charts and examines experiences endured by the soldiers. The collection contains more than a million fascinating objects, which includes armaments, prosthetics, maps and charts, clothing, uniforms, photos, books and vehicles. It also displays some more unusual artefacts like the skeleton of Napoleon's horse, Marengo; Florence Nightingale's paper lantern (*c.* 1856); and part of a telephone switchboard from Hitler's headquarters (*c.* 1944).

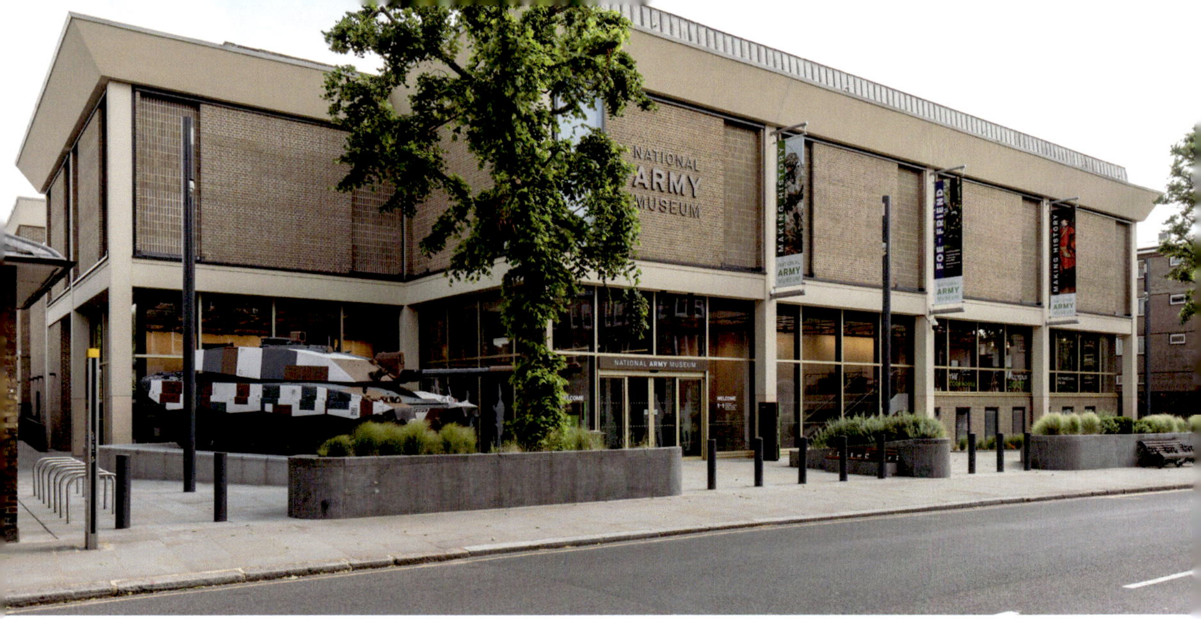

National Army Museum. (© James McCauley)

The museum is free to the public, has a café and shop and opens Tuesday to Sunday from 10 a.m. to 5.30 p.m.

www.nam.ac.uk

43. Royal Danish Embassy, Sloane Street, SW1

Often cited as a modernist masterpiece, the Danish Embassy certainly stands out in Sloane Street for its functional architectural style, so unlike much of the area. Built in 1977, it was designed by the prominent Danish architect Arne Jacobsen but was completed by the architects Dissing + Weitling after Jacobsen's death in 1971. It was a complex project as Jacobsen felt it important to ensure the embassy fitted in beside its neighbouring buildings that were of a much smaller scale. With this in mind, he designed a six-storey building facing Sloane Street where the upper two floors were recessed and the lower four floors jutted out to the height of the walls of the adjoining buildings. The sixth floor was from the start assigned as the ambassador's residence, while the fifth floor housed the ambassador's semi-private reception rooms. In his original plans Jacobsen proposed bronze plates on the façades and intended that that embassy would complement the surrounding buildings with its golden colour. However, budgetary constraints prevented this from happening and ultimately the exterior was painted and is now a much darker shade than Jacobsen had intended.

The main entrance to the embassy is on Sloane Street and is where people come to access the visa and information department and other chancellery functions. There is another entrance around the side in Hans Street, which leads to the

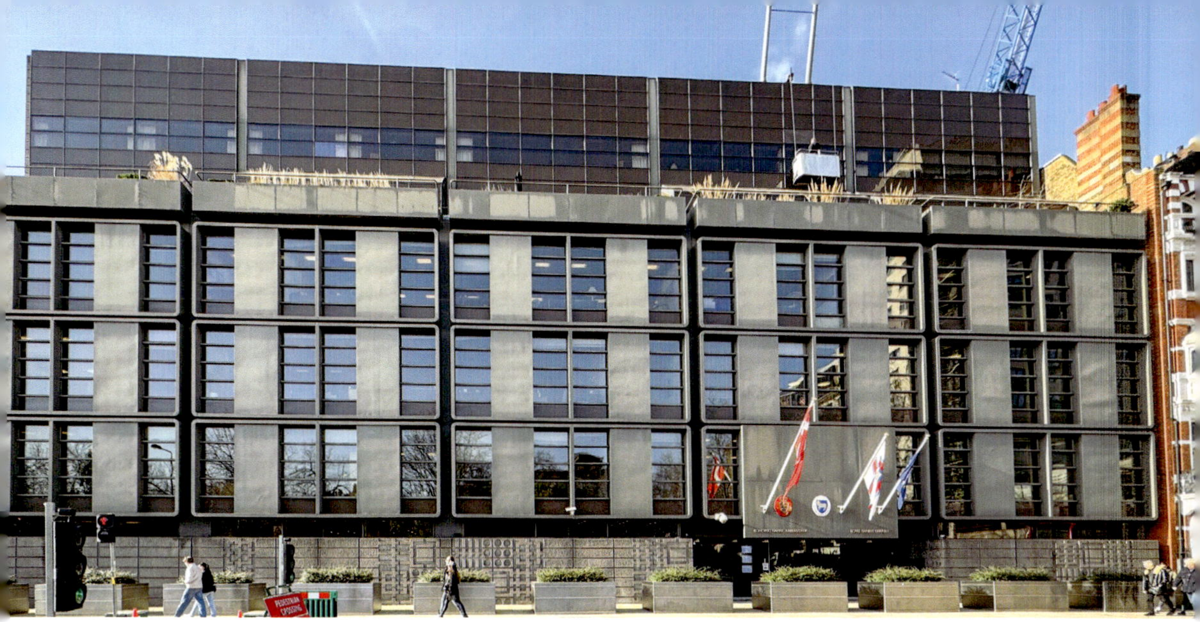

Royal Danish Embassy.

ambassador's residence and to a lecture and exhibition hall on the ground floor – today home to the Icelandic Embassy. Staff accommodation sits behind the main Embassy in a two-storey mews building.

www.storbritannien.um.dk

44. The Red House, No. 37 Tite Street, SW3

Located at the southern end of Tite Street close to the river, the Red House occupies a site near where the road bends across from Dilke Street. The property backs on to the grounds of the Royal Hospital Chelsea and although its style is entirely unique and quite dissimilar to other nearby houses, it appears to blend in with the urban landscape. Designed by Tony Fratton Architects and completed in 2002, the Red House was commissioned by the art collector heir to the Sainsbury family, Alex Sainsbury. He wanted a place where he could live and work that would work well as a family home and as a space to display his vast collection of contemporary art. The house exterior, clad in red French limestone, is warm in hue but its unadorned façade can seem stark, austere and even unwelcoming at first glance. In contrast, the interior is a great deal more opulent, furnishings are superbly crafted, and the materials used of the highest quality. The designers have provided a spacious interior – there is a stunning double-height salon on the first floor with windows that fills the room with light. The room itself is almost a double cube in shape and looks out on to the entrance court and rear garden. The bedrooms are situated beside the roof garden at the top of the house while the kitchen along with other domestic rooms fill the ground-floor living space. Tony Fretton is renowned for being a good listener, picking up on his clients' requirements and ensuring he gives

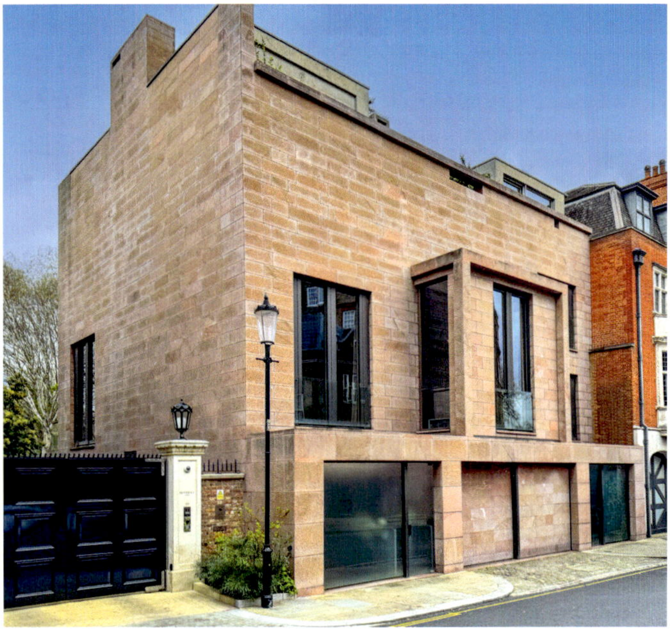

The Red House.

them what they want. In the case of the Red House, despite its somewhat box-like exterior he has managed to produce an interior containing a series of spaces that are highly functional, relaxed, stylish and work well together.

45. Chelsea Harbour and Imperial Wharf, SW10

The land that Chelsea Harbour occupies today was owned from the early 1800s by the Imperial Gas Light and Coke Company. Although very successful (by the mid-nineteenth century the company had become London's foremost gas company) the introduction of North Sea gas in the 1970s caused the gasworks to close, which resulted in the land becoming derelict and subsequently available for redevelopment.

Almost thirty years has passed since planning permission was granted to develop Chelsea Harbour. Built beside Chelsea Creek on the border between the Royal Borough of Kensington & Chelsea and the Borough of Hammersmith & Fulham, it was to be one of the largest construction projects the UK had initiated for many decades and one that revitalised the south-western part of the Thames in London. Designed by the architects Moxley Jenner & Partners, it was planned as a mixed-use development comprising luxury residential accommodation, a five-star hotel, the Chelsea Harbour Marina and the Chelsea Harbour Design Centre.

The art historian Nikolaus Pevsner describes Chelsea Harbour as 'An instant riverside town for the rich', and with its luxury yachts and speedboats, manicured gardens and landscaping, expensive apartments and upmarket hotel this is

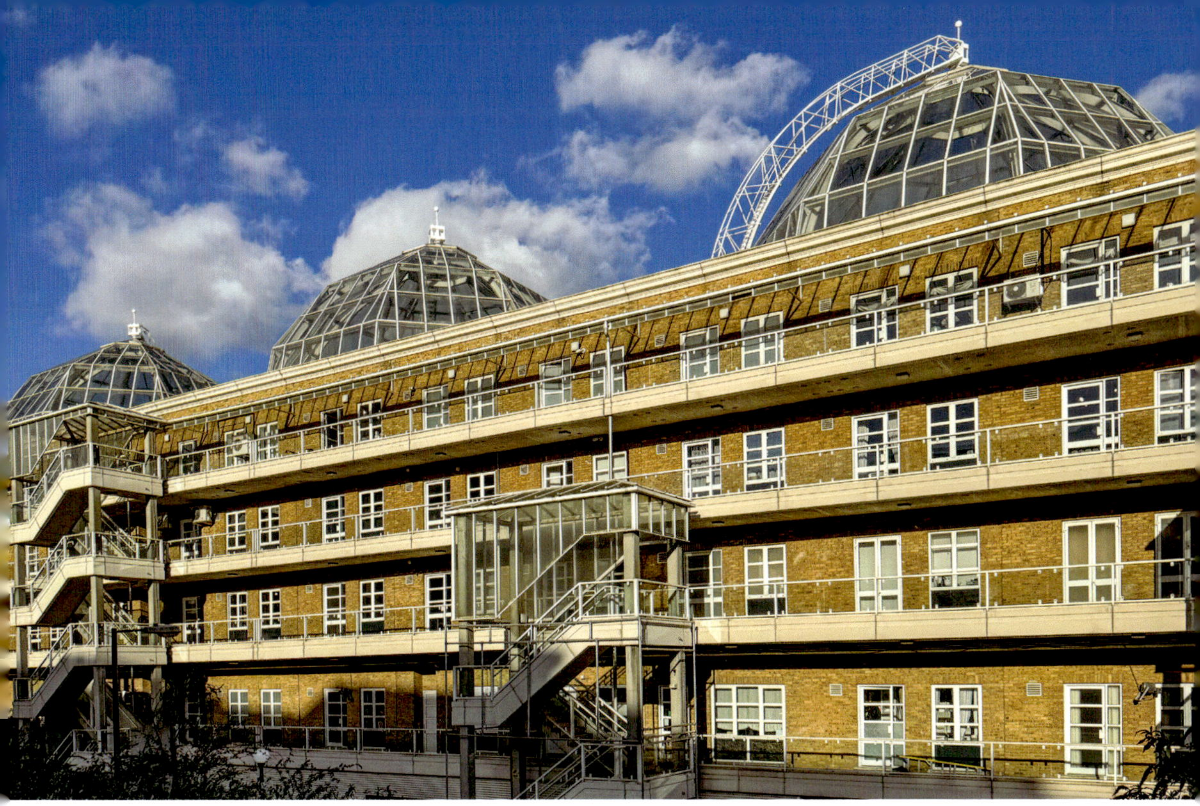

Above: The Chelsea Design Centre.

Below: Chelsea Harbour.

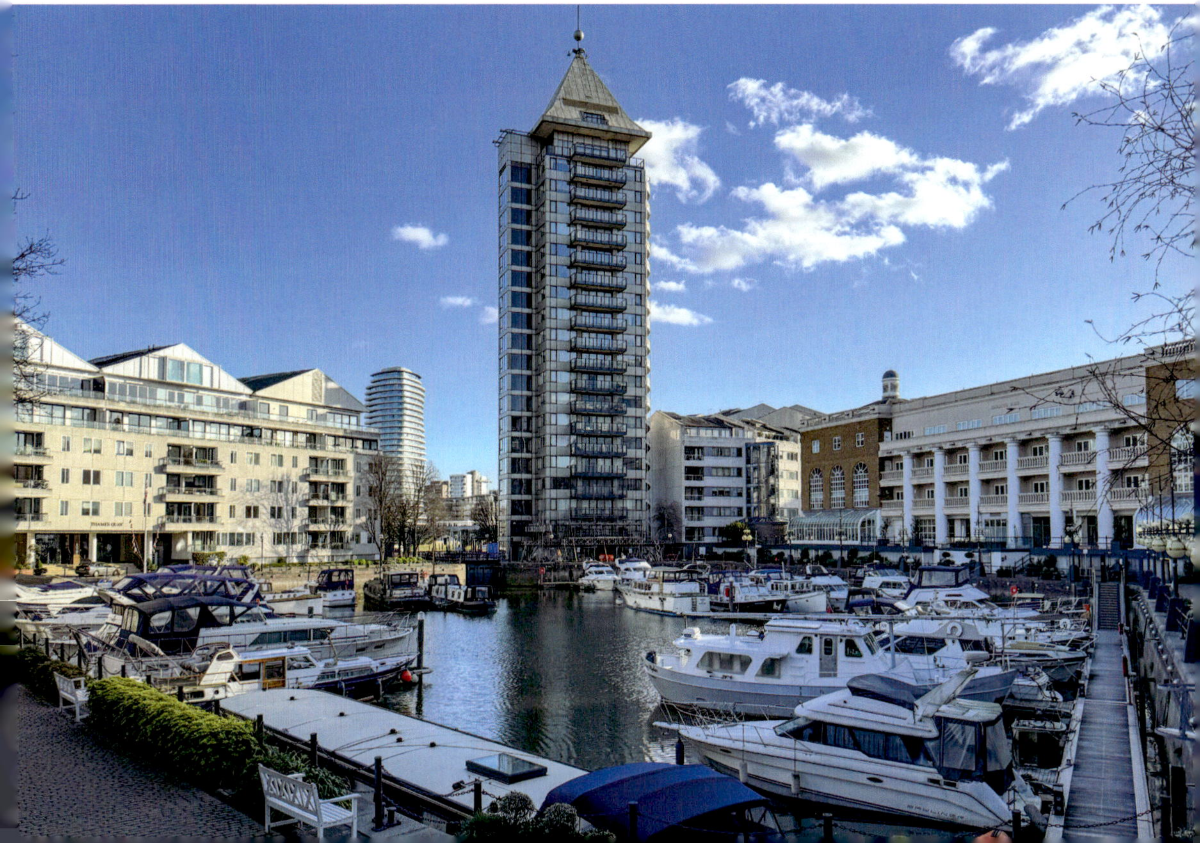

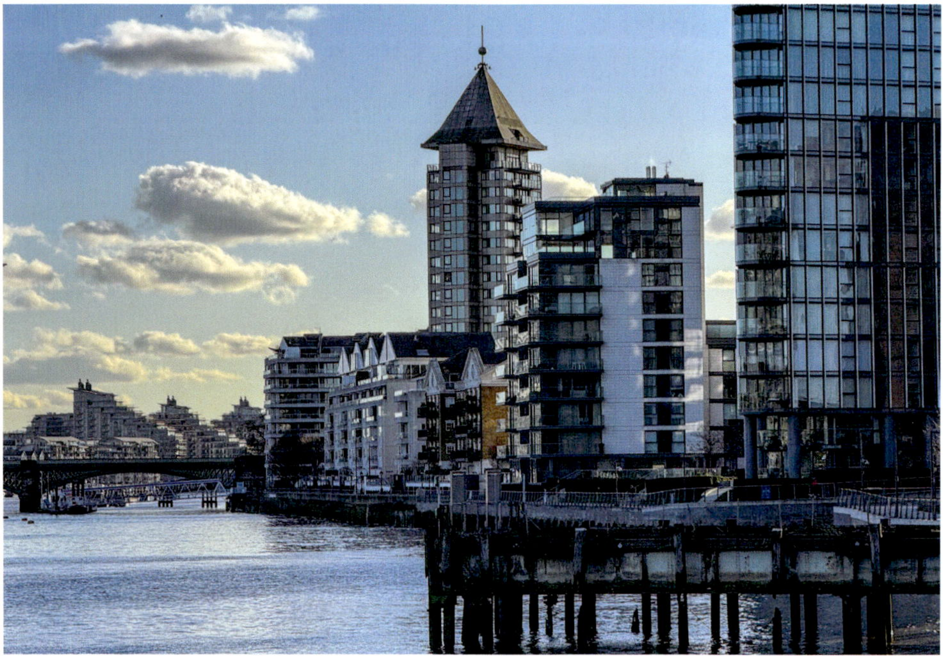

Imperial Wharf.

probably not far from the truth. Naturally, it has resulted in residents of some note, including Sir Michael Caine, Robbie Williams, Tom Stoppard, Sally Burton and Sir Ralph Halpern and attracts many visiting celebrities too. A second riverside apartment complex, Imperial Wharf, began construction in the early 2000s. This development contains even more luxury riverside apartments and has ultimately brought about the creation of a new train station, also Imperial Wharf, to the area. The complex itself has continued to grow, and its fine restaurants, gorgeous riverside views, shops, bars and cafés make this an increasingly popular venue.

Another treasure of the area is the Chelsea Design Centre, which describes itself as 'the world's premier destination for design and decoration'. Located in an impressive glass-domed building it is filled with designer showrooms and is a magnificent resource for professional designers and architects working on major domestic and commercial projects. The centre opens from 9.30 a.m. to 5.30 p.m. Monday to Friday.

46. King's Road Cinemas, SW3

Few people walking along the King's Road are probably aware of its association with film, but glance up at the façade of The Gaumont (Nos 196–222 King's Road) and you will see a ceramic plaque with the face of William Friese-Greene, an early pioneer and inventor of the moving image. It was here in his laboratory and studio that Friese-Green experimented with photographs and cinematography. When his

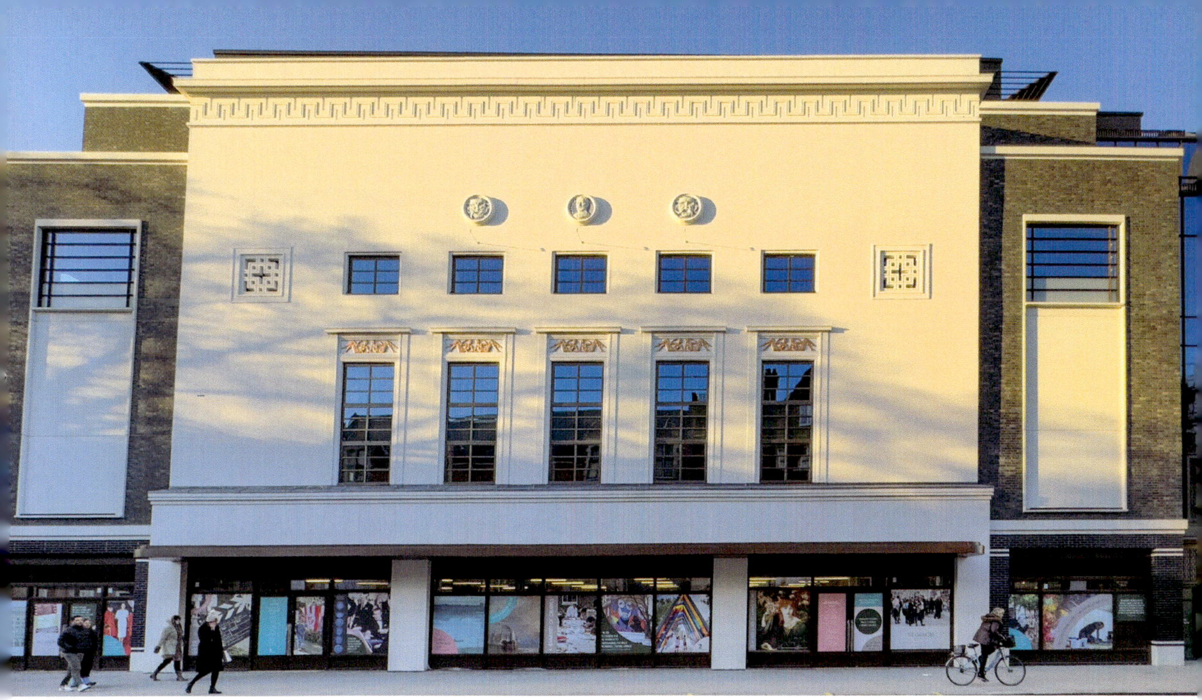

Above: The Gaumont.

Right: Façade details on the Gaumont.

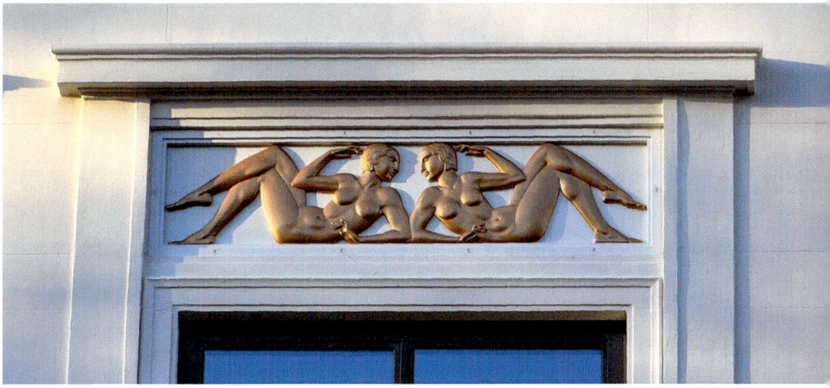

funeral took place in 1921 his coffin was topped with a model of a film projector pointing at a screen inscribed with the words, 'The End'.

The Gaumont, at Nos 206–208 King's Road, opened in 1934 as a cinema named the Gaumont Palace. The cinema has changed its name many times in the intervening years and after it closed in 1972 the building was converted into the Habitat store at No. 208, and the Odeon cinema moved into smaller premises at No 206, part of the former cinema. For nearly twenty years it has been run by the Curzon group, but the cinema and adjacent buildings underwent a massive redevelopment recently as Cadogan Estates, the landowner, decided to transform the site into a commercial and cultural hub. The new independent Curzon cinema is part of a mixed-use development that includes, luxury flats, a rooftop bar with wonderful panoramic views of London, offices, a large pub, a Waitrose store, retail space and four retail units dedicated for use by Chelsea's creatives. The art deco façade has not only been restored but has also been enhanced by a permanent artwork, hand-sculpted from ceramic tiles by the artist, Shezad Dawood.

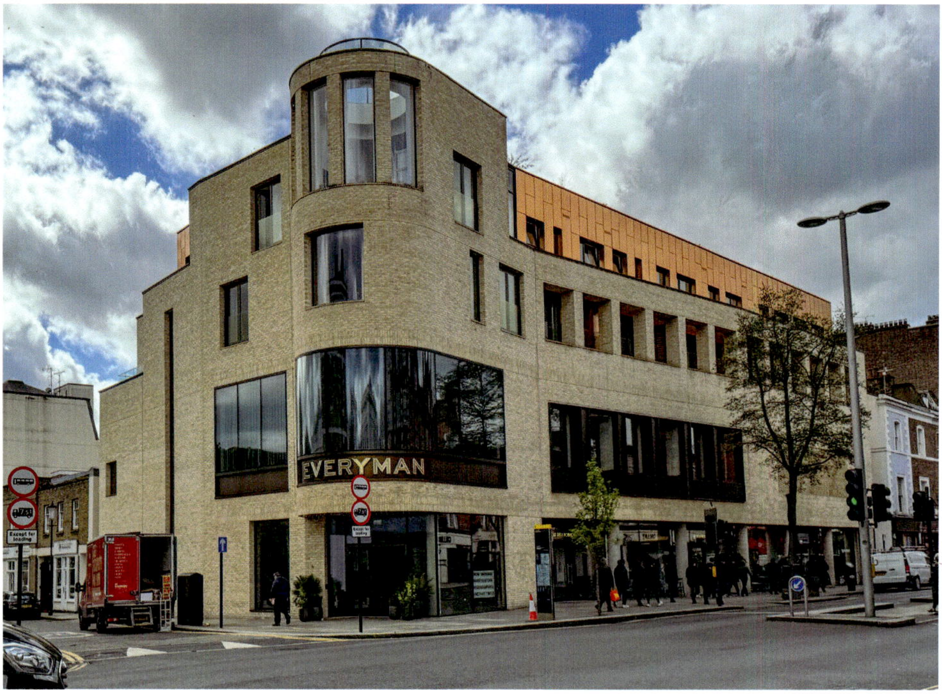

The Everyman cinema.

Just a few blocks west at Nos 279–281 is another popular cinema, nowadays run by the Everyman group. Like the Gaumont the Everyman Chelsea has seen many reincarnations since it first appeared as the Palaseum in 1910. By 1912 it was known as the King's Picture House and later renamed, first as the Ritz and then the Essoldo. In 1980 it re-opened with four screens as the Classic Cinema. Nowadays, The Everyman Chelsea is a plush three-screen cinema. There is a deluxe bar and lounge area in the foyer and wine and food are served to your seat.

www.thegaumont.co.uk
www.everymancinema.com

47. Pavilion Road, SW1

In 2015 the Cadogan Estate held a consultation with the local community to discover what Chelsea residents and workers wanted in their neighbourhood. It became clear from the discussions that residents felt it would be of great benefit to themselves and enhance the village atmosphere of Chelsea if an area could be established for independent shops selling quality produce. This resulted in the redevelopment of what was originally a back street, Pavilion Road, into what has now become a foodie's paradise. The street, which is easily accessed from Sloane Square and the King's Road,

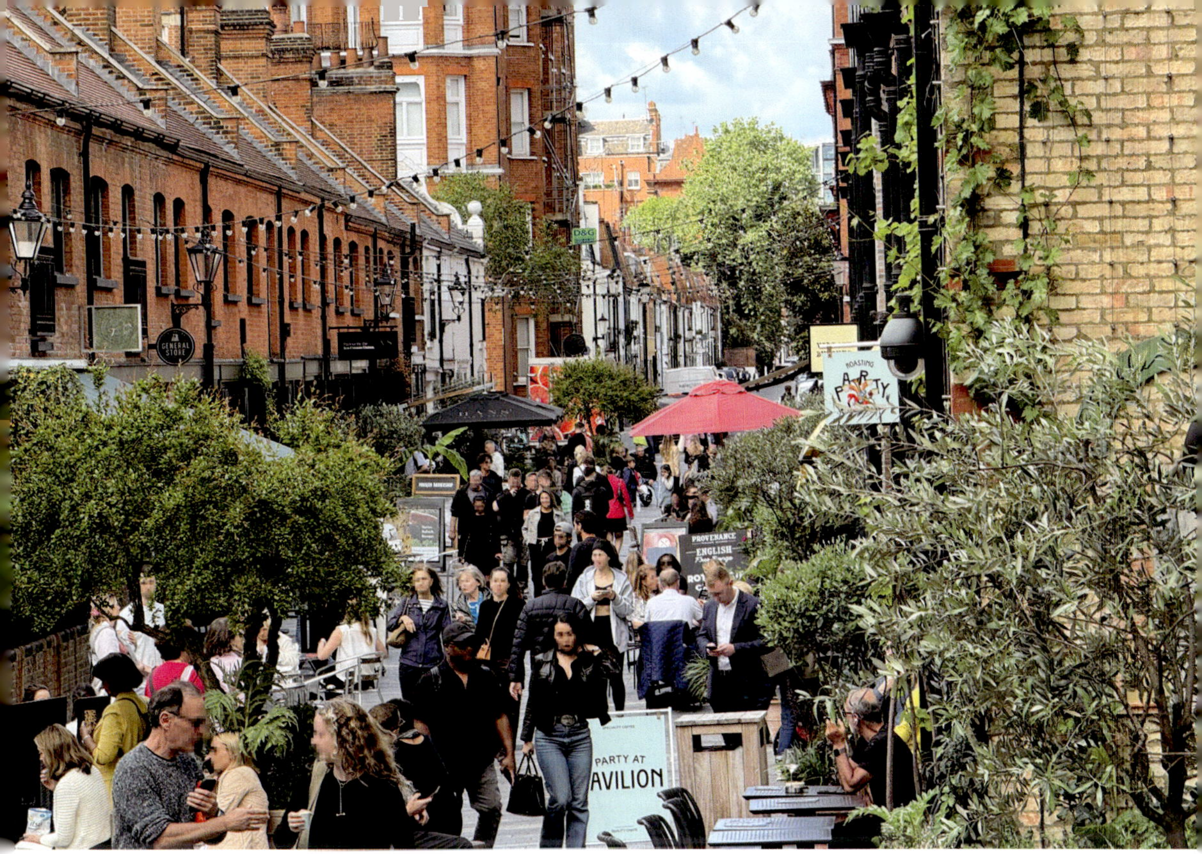

Above and below: Pavilion Road.

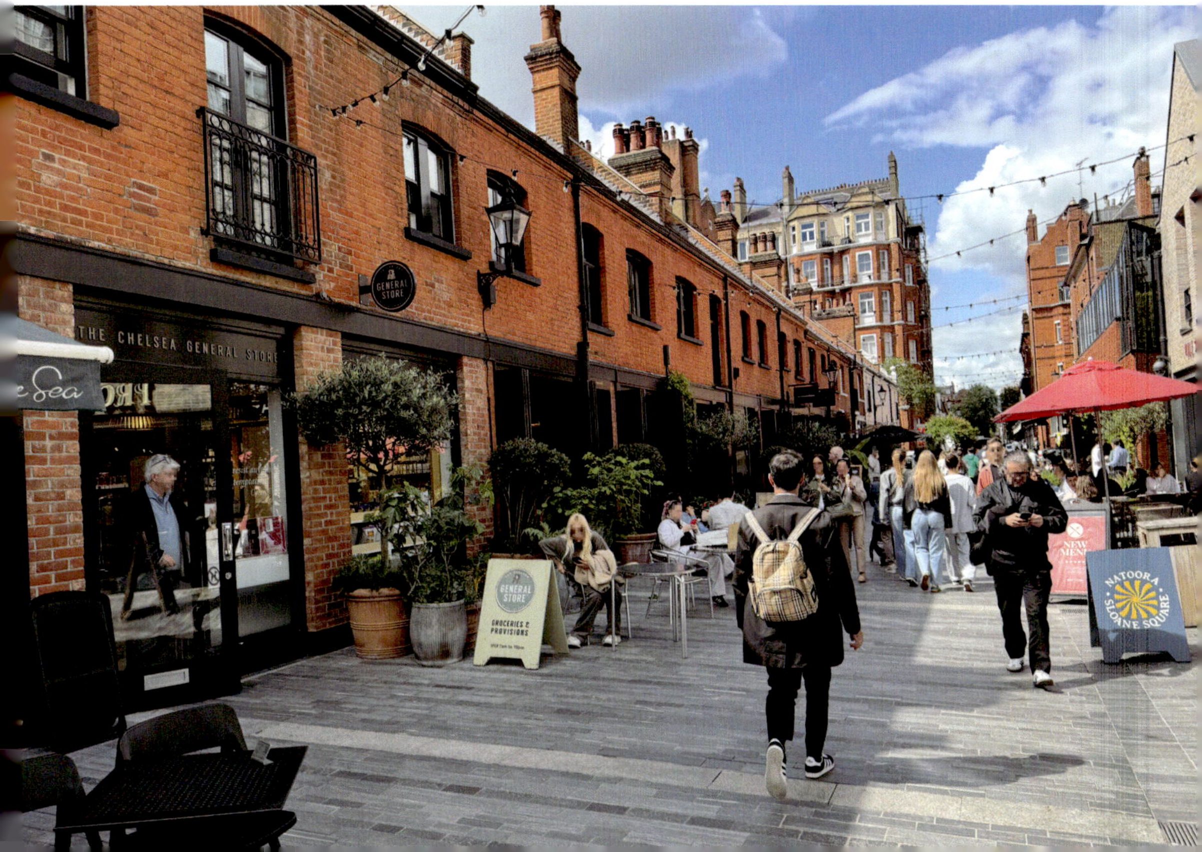

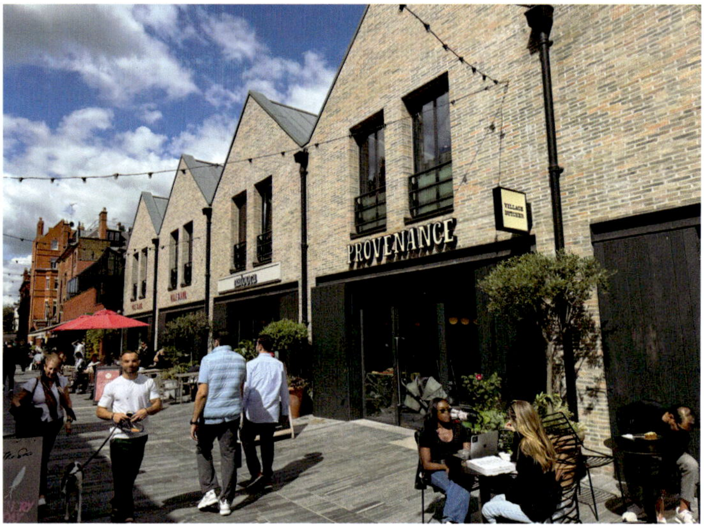

Pavilion Road.

runs parallel to Sloane Street and claims to be London's longest mews. Unimpeded by traffic (it is pedestrianised at the southern end) it is filled with street cafés and restaurants, making this a real gourmet quarter of Chelsea. Al fresco dining and people watching are major activities on Pavilion Road and it stays busy here all day long.

In addition to providing a new area to eat, Cadogan Estate has attracted a fantastic range of artisanal shops to Pavilion Road, which has resulted in a high-class butcher, baker, greengrocer, wine merchant and cheesemonger, among others. Cadogan Estate has transformed what was previously more of a cut-through road into a delightfully picturesque area that is now full of greenery and is beautifully landscaped. Moreover, the nineteenth-century homes and red-brick architecture of the street have been thoughtfully blended with the new contemporary building of George House, which lies between Pavilion Road and Sloane Street.

48. Vardo, Duke of York Square, SW3

Vardo opened in September 2019 and has been another great success for the Cadogan Estate. It is part of the Caravan Coffee Roasters group and styles itself as a 'nomadic all day dining concept'. The final part of the Duke of York Square development to be completed the restaurant's indoor-outdoor dining experience has proved to be remarkably popular. Housed in a striking circular stone and glass pavilion that is surrounded by the Saatchi Art Gallery, a sports field, the King's Road and the Duke of York Square, Vardo has full-height glazing that retracts into basement trenches when the weather is warm. Its designers, Nex, have pioneered the very first retractable curved glass system worldwide (although there are similar straight panel systems elsewhere), which comes in very useful in a country where the weather can be somewhat unpredictable.

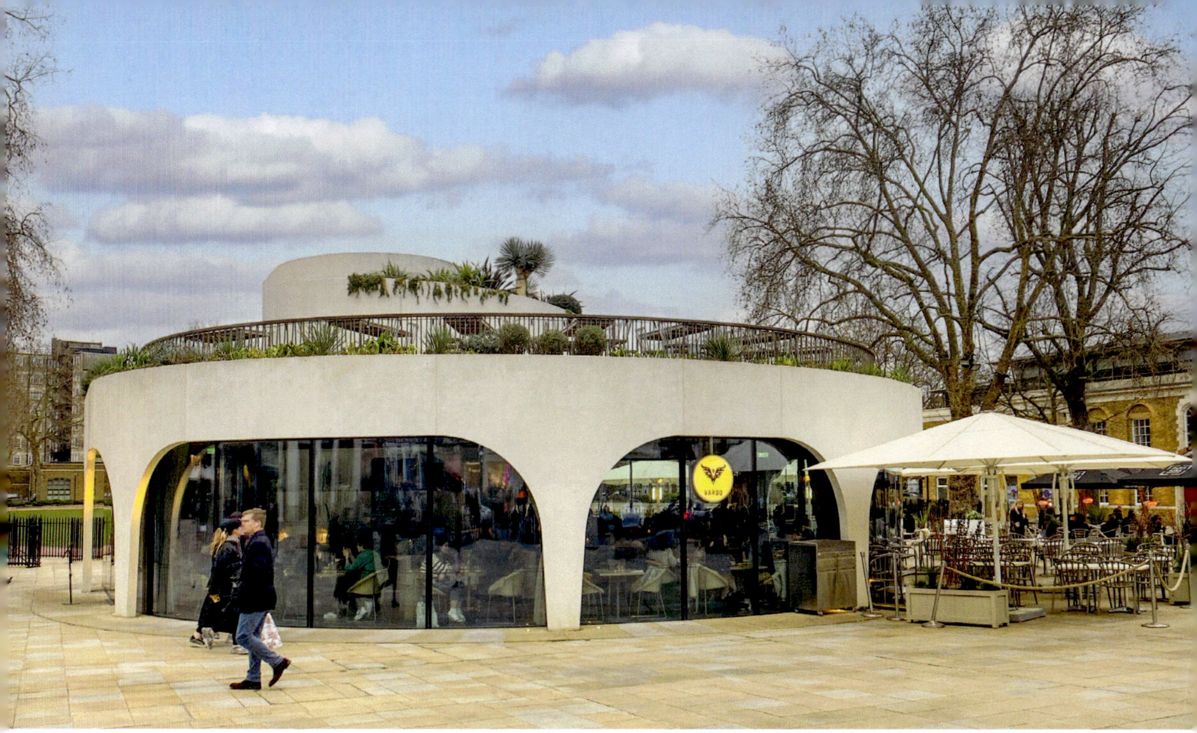

Above and right: Vardo.

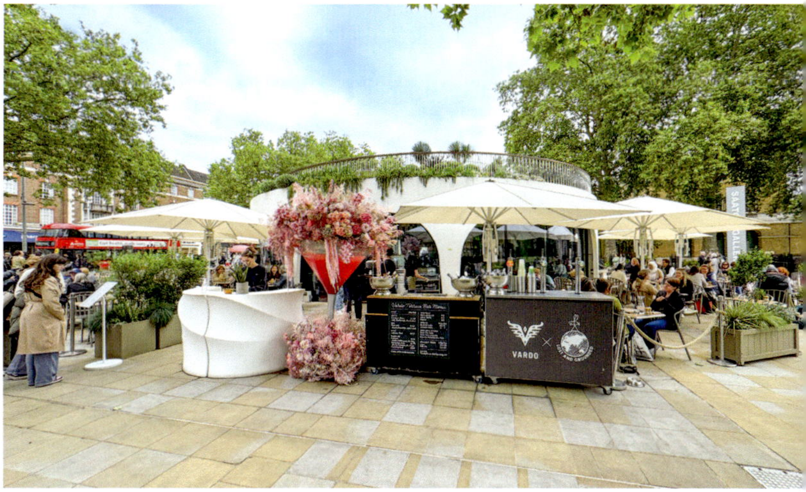

Nex won Cadogan Estate's international competition to create a contemporary restaurant in the square and the building they have designed is both unusual and wonderfully accessible. The architects have produced a 360-degree structure that feels open but also contains intimate spaces. All the services are placed in the basement area while above the restaurant is a stunning hidden roof garden. This is accessed via an attractive spiral staircase and open to the public.

Vardo's restaurant is undoubtedly a dynamic building that both complements its surroundings and has also become a landmark on the King's Road.

www.caravanandco.com

49. Chelsea Barracks, Chelsea Bridge Road, SW1

For more than 130 years Chelsea Barracks was home to soldiers of the British Army. The original barracks constructed in 1862 were built in a long line only interrupted by towers in the middle and housed members of the infantry. In the 1960s these buildings were demolished and replaced by two thirteen-storey tower blocks which provided accommodation for four companies from the Guards Regiment, the Grenadier, Irish, Welsh and Scots Guards. The Ministry of Defence decided to sell off the barracks in the early 2000s, citing the need for expensive and extensive renovation to the buildings. By 2008 the soldiers had been relocated to Woolwich and the barracks sold off to a consortium. Subsequently the entire site was taken over by Qatari Diar, who after several years managed to obtain planning permission to develop the site for residential housing. Designs for the buildings by Squire and Partners were finally approved, with construction of the first phase commencing in 2015.

Although not yet complete, a substantial part of the Chelsea Barracks housing development has now been built. It offers luxurious townhouses as well as contemporary blocks of apartments and exclusive penthouses, many of which are located around public garden squares. During the 2024 Chelsea Flower Show

Chelsea Barracks.

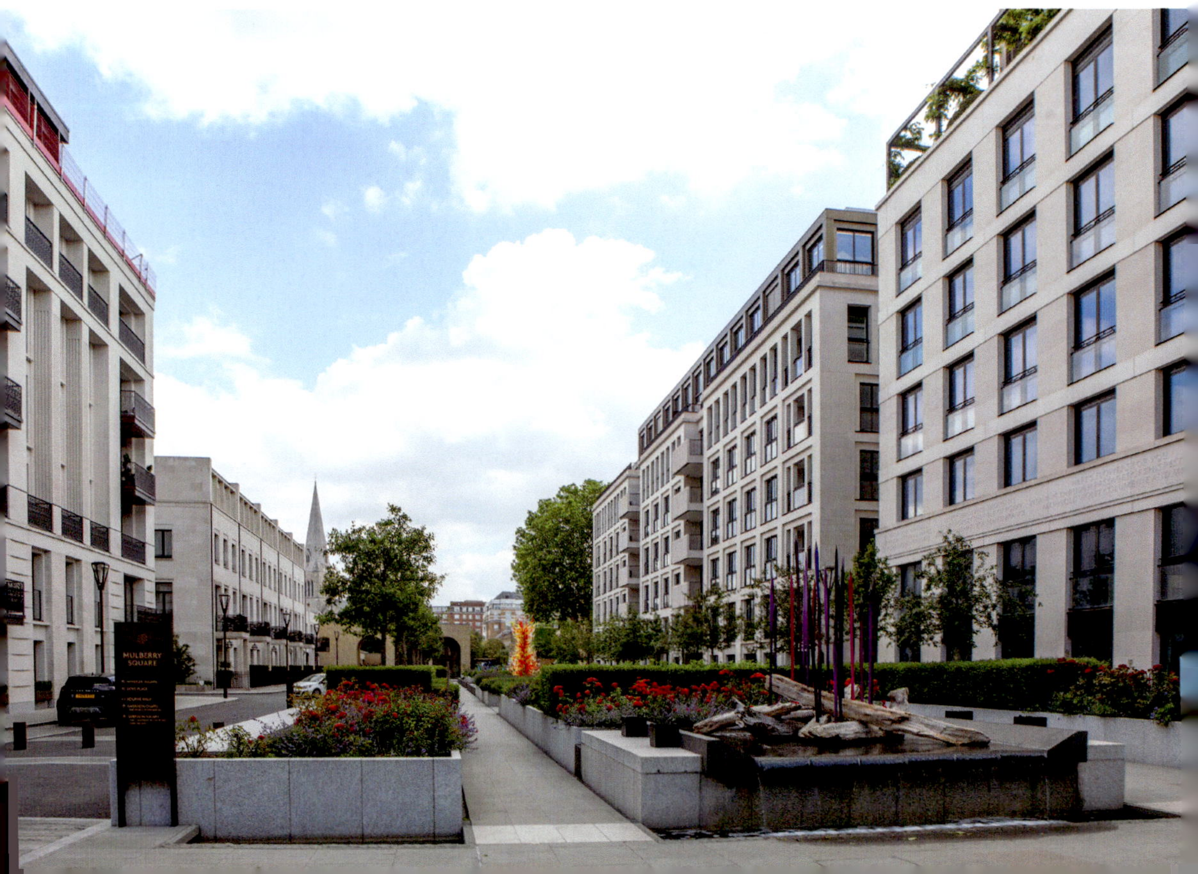

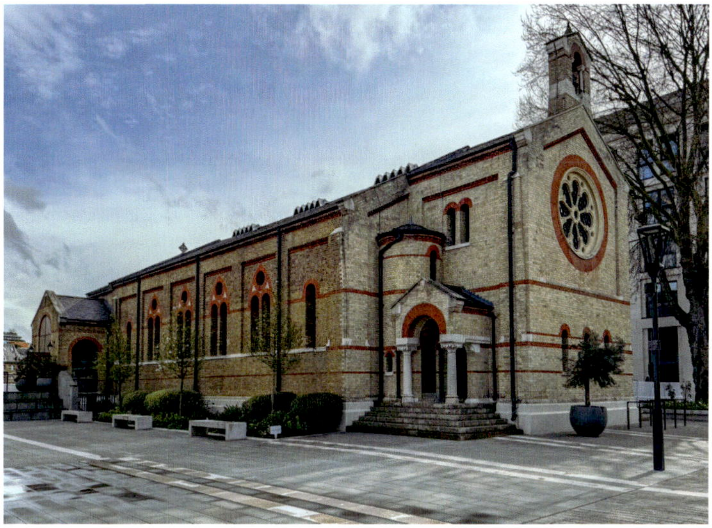

Royal Garrison Chapel.

Mulberry Square, the main entrance to the estate was decorated with a most striking display of glass sculptures by the American glass artist Dale Chihuly.

The one Victorian building to remain on the site is the Grade II listed Garrison Chapel, which has undergone a superb restoration. Today home to the King's Foundation, it stages exhibitions and showcases the work of the charity. The magnificent building boasts original floor mosaics, Corinthian columns and a spectacular wooden strutted roof.

www.chelseabarracks.com

50. Powerhouse at Chelsea Waterfront (former Lots Road Power Station), SW10

Like many buildings across London, the Lots Road Power Station has undergone a total transformation in recent years. The original power station, characterised by its four enormous chimneys (now two), multitude of windows and warm red-brick exterior began its working life in 1905 and for almost 100 years it generated electricity to power the entire London Underground network from its base beside the Thames. It was one of the largest steel-framed buildings in the country and quickly became a true icon of the area. The station used 700 tonnes of coal each day, which was delivered by river barges from a purpose-built tidal basin at Chelsea Creek and from the nearby West London Railway. Later the power station was powered by both coal and oil, and for a short while by gas when oil prices soared in the 1970s. London Transport has produced numerous posters of the power station, one of which describes it as being 'the moving spirit of London'. The building was finally decommissioned in 2002, at which point the National Grid took over its role.

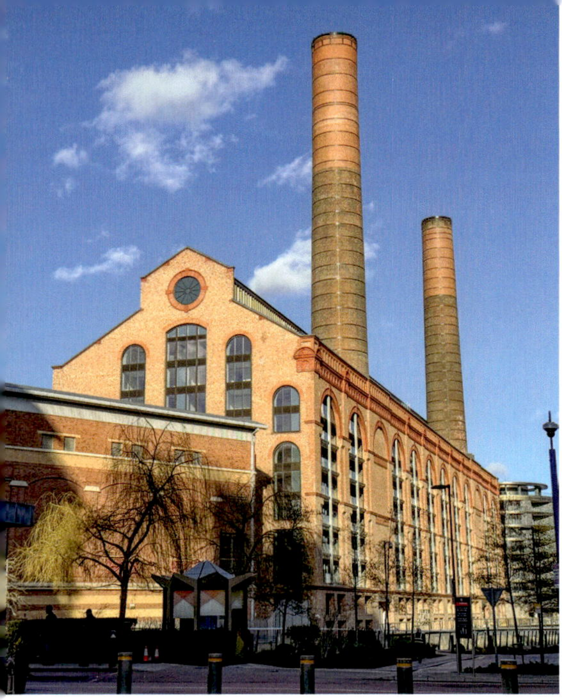

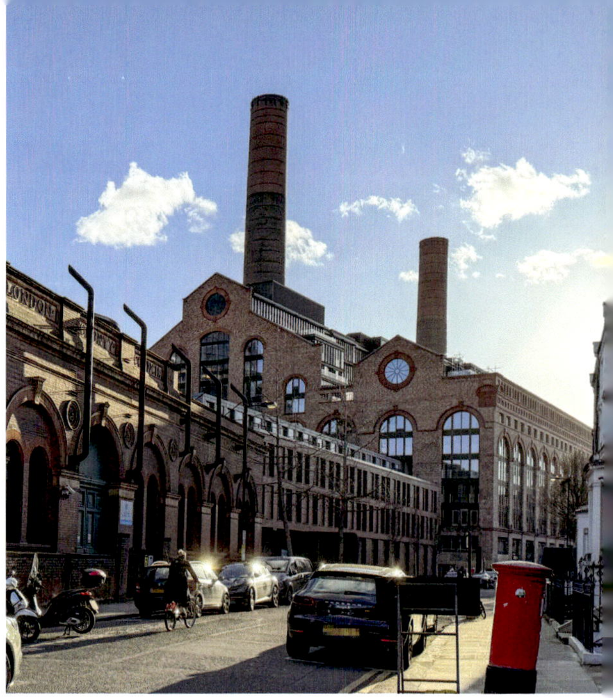

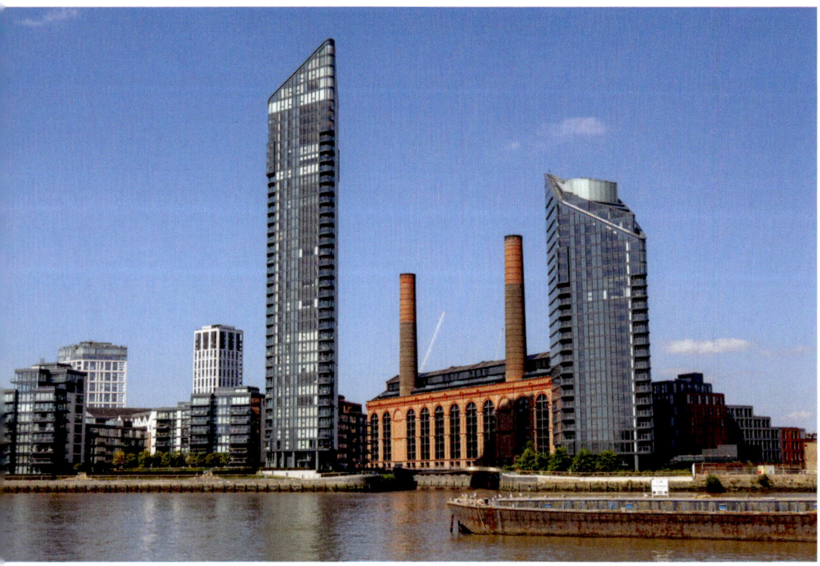

Above left, above right and left: Powerhouse at Chelsea Waterfront.

Now, after a massive restoration, the power station has been converted into exclusive apartments and is part of the Chelsea Waterfront development that consists of two glass residential tower blocks and three riverside buildings. New bridges spanning the creek connect the buildings and the developers have created wonderful gardens and paths beside the river. The power station has been renamed 'Powerhouse' and with its cathedral-like appearance, fabulous architecture and stunning windows, it certainly lives up to its new name.

www.powerhousechelsea.com

Acknowledgements

The author would like to thank all the people and organisations that have facilitated the production of this book. In particular to acknowledge the help and assistance given by Chelsea Old Church, Chelsea Physic Garden, Crosby Moran Hall, Royal Hospital Chelsea, No. Fifty Cheyne, St Luke's and Christchurch, The Cadogan Arms, The Cadogan Hotel, Chelsea Old Town Hall, Holy Trinity Church, Michelin House, Most Holy Redeemer Church, Cadogan Hall, The Bluebird, and the National Army Museum.

I cannot emphasise enough the enormous role played by my husband, Alex McMurdo, whose many images adorn the book. He has been a continual support whilst the book was being written and has accompanied me on numerous walks along the streets of Chelsea. Please note that all images displayed without credit are his work and copyright. I am further indebted to him and Jo for taking the time to proofread the text, for their feedback and constructive criticism.

I would like to take this opportunity too to thank Amberley Publishing for commissioning the book, and to acknowledge the excellent support and hard work of Jenny Bennett, Nick Grant, Becky Cadenhead and all the team.

About the Author

Lucy McMurdo is a modern history graduate and native Londoner who has lived in the capital all her life. In 2003 when she qualified as a London Blue Badge Tourist Guide she combined two of her major loves – history and London – and has been sharing her knowledge of the city with locals and visitors ever since. Always keen to explore and learn about London's secrets, she spends many hours 'walking the streets' looking out for hidden corners, unusual curiosities as well as architecturally significant buildings and ones that have a story to tell.

Lucy's tour guiding career began over forty years ago when she first guided overseas visitors around the UK. Since then, in addition to tour guiding she has been greatly involved in training and examining the next generation of tour guides. She has created, taught and run courses in London's University of Westminster and City University, and also developed guide-training programmes for the warders and site guides at Hampton Court Palace.

Most recently Lucy has been writing about the city she is so passionate about and is the author of ten London books: *Shoreditch and Hoxton in 50 Buildings*, *Secret Islington and Clerkenwell*, *Southwark and Blackfriars in 50 Buildings*, *The City of London in 50 Buildings*, *Highgate and Hampstead in 50 Buildings*, *Islington and Clerkenwell in 50 Buildings*, *Chiswick in 50 Buildings*, *Bloomsbury in 50 Buildings*, *Explore London's Square Mile*, *Streets of London* and *London in 7 Days*.